FROM HOBBY TO OBSESSION

FROM HOBBY TO OBSESSION

Darragh MacAnthony

© Neil Gilby, 2012

Published by The Posh Book Company
www.theposhbookcompany.co.uk

A CIP catalogue record for this book is available from the British Library.

ISBN 978-0-9573024-0-2

Cover design by Neil Gilby and Chris Brewer

Prepared by:

York Publishing Services Ltd
64 Hallfield Road
Layerthorpe
York YO31 7ZQ

Tel: 01904 431213

Website: www.yps-publishing.co.uk

Printed and bound in the U.K.

I dedicate this book to my incredible wife Natalie and my three beautiful children Calum, Cara and Darci.

ACKNOWLEDGEMENTS

A massive special mention must go to Neil Gilby who without his time, patience, persistence and dedication, this book would never have happened.

Neil works for Peterborough United Football Club and through seeing what an asset he is to my football club, I approached him about the idea of writing a book and from there on in, he is the man who made it happen.

Neil you are not just an employee or a fan, you are a true friend. Thank you Cornelius!!!

CONTENTS

FOREWORD

It feels like yesterday when I first decided to buy a football club and enter the sports world in what was to be a hobby for me and a nice distraction away from the daily grind of business interests and 24/7 travel on work-related matters. As a 30-year-old football-mad person, I was about to embark on a journey that 99% of most football fans would love to take. I never ignore the fact that I live most people's dreams and am very grateful to be in this position. I never take it for granted.

When I became Chairman of Peterborough United Football Club, who were a mid-table League Two side just over six years ago, little did I know that this hobby of mine would include:

- Investing over £11 million pounds of my own money

- Hiring the son of one of football's most famous, if not the most famous, manager in the game today, Sir Alex Ferguson

- Going to war over becoming owner of the club for twelve long months

- Experiencing three promotions over five seasons

- Experiencing the depression of relegation

- Seeing my team score over four hundred goals in the process

- Going through five different managers in such a short space of time, thus effectively making me Number 1 hatchet Chairman according to 442 magazine

- Seeing my club upset the odds and compete comfortably in the Championship

- Upsetting so many opposition fans, like I did the Huddersfield supporters

- Signing over sixty-plus new players

- Selling and paying off many more

- Making thousands of people happy on so many occasions

- Falling foul of the FA and getting fined

- Dealing with so many agents, both qualified and unqualified

- Bringing in Posh's first £1 million player

- Seeing the pressure of winning a football game practically give me a heart attack

- Becoming obsessed about making Posh a football club to be envied by other football clubs and their fans for succeeding with the right ideals and policies

This book will lead you through the journey over the last six exciting, often rollercoaster, years with the good, the bad, the ugly, but above all the TRUTH about what it's really like to own a football club and everything that goes with it. Trust me when I say that a hobby it is not: it is an outright obsession and one that affects my everyday life for better or worse. There is nothing I would change as I believe everything that happens in life is an education, which leads me to quote my favourite saying: 'We are all allowed to make mistakes, just as long as we never make the same mistake twice.' Enjoy the read, the journey, the highs and lows; enjoy the real side to the football world as experienced by me.

Darragh MacAnthony
Chairman, Peterborough United Football Club

HOW IT STARTED

Let's go back to 1986, when I was ten. In my house, in the south side of Dublin, rugby was the sport and second to that was golf. Football (soccer, as it was formally known round our way) was nowhere to be seen. I played a lot of rugby as a child. I never kicked a football in my life, but rugby was perfect for me. By the age of fourteen I was 6'2, I was a second row and a number 8 and I went on to captain one of my local teams. As time went by the clubs around me started looking for commitment, and I was more interested in clubbing and girls. I decided I needed to pick one of the two, and it wasn't rugby!

So that's when my sports career stopped.

But back at the age of ten it was all rugby – my dad would take me to all the Irish games, and I would regularly watch my local team, St. Mary's, play. Soccer was on TV and in my area it was always looked down upon and considered more for the lower class, and rugby for the upper class. That's just how it was.

When I eventually got into soccer I think it must have broken my dad's heart, because he certainly never had a love for the game. I remember we went out for lunch one Sunday afternoon, and it actually happened to be the day of the 1988 FA cup final. My parents used to enjoy a few bottles of wine after lunch, and chill whilst we kids played and charged around. I remember there was a small TV in the corner and on that TV was a soccer match between a red team and a blue team (it was in fact Liverpool v Wimbledon), which I started to watch. My dad came over and asked what I was watching, and I told him it was a soccer match. He rolled his eyes and asked me who I wanted to win, and I said the team in blue! Now my Dad's not a football fan but he knew that out of Liverpool and Wimbledon, Liverpool would win any day. Everyone knew the success that Liverpool was having around that time. 'I'll bet you a tenner that the red team win,' my dad said, which I took him up on and in so doing made my first bet. Fortunately for me Wimbledon pulled off a shock and won the game 1-0 and I was ten pounds up.

Suddenly, from that day on, I had a bug on soccer and became fixated on it, to the point where I would support a team in every division and then go out and buy the papers to find out how each team had done over the weekend. I became obsessed with Liverpool. Even though the reds lost that day, my allegiance afterwards lay with them and it hasn't changed since. Ironically enough the FA cup match was not my first flirtation with Liverpool FC, during the 80's myself and my family used to go to Spain for ten weeks on holiday, and we were very fortunate in being able to do this. We went to an exclusive resort called Playas Del Duque in Puerto Banus. Every day that summer these two Scottish guys would be out on the grass with two kids, using trees as goals. The girl was called Kelly and the boy was called Paul; they were brother and sister and their surname was Dalglish.

Obviously Kelly went on to be a Sky Sports presenter and Paul, I think, manages an MLS team out in the states. In fact Kelly may not remember this but my first ever peck on the cheek was from Kelly Dalglish, so that's a claim to fame (for her of course!). The two Scottish gentleman were their dad Kenny, who was Liverpool player/manager at the time, and his best mate Alan Hanson, who of course is a Liverpool legend. These two guys invited me every day whilst we were there together to come and play football with them all. It was fantastic. They were a lovely family and Alan Hanson was a top bloke.

I moved to Spain in the '90s, and by this time Graeme Souness was in charge. He didn't do much whilst managing the club but what he did do was introduce young talent into the club like Redknapp and Fowler from the youth team into the first team, and that's what needed to happen because Liverpool hadn't really developed their own players in the past. Under Dalglish they relied on the best players from lower leagues and developed them, like John Barnes and Ray Houghton.

Back then that's what top clubs used to do – they wouldn't think twice in buying League Two's best winger, whereas these days you don't really see that happen any more, which is a shame. Nobody really likes to take a gamble, but back then, for Liverpool, it paid off big time.

I was never able to get to any Liverpool matches growing up. Because my dad wasn't a football fan, he wasn't going to take me to any soccer match, and with myself not being able to afford to travel, it just wasn't feasible for me. In fact the first Liverpool match I went to watch was in 2002 against Everton for the Merseyside Derby. It finished 0-0 but the next one I went to see made up for it.

It was Istanbul, Turkey, the greatest European Cup final in modern years against Italian giants Milan. We were 3-0 down at half time and I was beginning to think I was a jinx. Then in the second half Liverpool came out and brought it back to 3-3, and then it went to penalties, which of course Liverpool went on to win. So a great occasion to watch my first Liverpool victory with my own eyes. I followed this up by going to the rematch in Greece a couple of years later but left disappointed after a dull Benitez team selection ended in a 2-0 defeat.

MY WISH LIST

One thing I have always been big into is targets, setting myself goals. When I started my first business back in 1999/2000 I drew up a list of things I wanted: a Ferrari, a big home, a nice watch, a million pounds in the bank... And each year I would add to this list: travel on a private jet, go on nice holidays, etc. By 2005 I had pretty much accomplished everything on my wish list.

So by the end of that year I added 'own a football club' to that list. It had got to the stage where I was making so much money that I sat back and thought, What would be the ultimate hobby, the ultimate dream? And it had come to me that buying my own football club would tick that box. Now obviously I couldn't afford to buy Liverpool, but I could afford to buy a football club – just not one in the higher reaches of English football.

Everyone around me was saying, 'Are you crazy? You don't even live in the UK, how can you run a football club?' Now, what people don't realise is that when you're making so much money – and I mean a serious amount of money – you feel invincible, like nothing is impossible. So the idea of buying a football club in England and running it from abroad – in my arrogance it seemed easy, a piece of piss, or so I thought at the time. Ah, to be young and stupid, I hear you say!

Unfortunately, around that time my mother passed away. I also broke up from a relationship, fell in love with Natalie, got married, started a family – and I got distracted from buying a football club.

But there came a time, in the summer of 2006, when I would go into the office and my eyes would keep getting drawn to that list and the unticked box. I eventually thought, Right, I'm going to do it, I'm in a good place at work and at home and it will be a great hobby, not to mention a great release away from the stresses and rigors of normal life. I'm not a big drinker, I don't really socialise and there were never any big hobbies in my life. Golf I love, but I was never going to play that every day.

I thought it would cost me £500,000 a year to run a football club, which I could easily manage to do and then I would have a club I could call my own. I'm not one to seek permission from my family, as they trust me and my judgments and know that whatever I do will be right for the them long-term, and this would be a great release for me.

You have to remember that at that time I was doing forty weekends a year travelling. That's what I did, and it was coming to the point where I had over a thousand staff worldwide working in the business, including a large board of directors running the day-to-day operations, so it allowed me to step back and begin to enjoy myself. My plans were to buy a football club for around £1 million and then drip-feed it with money every now and again. Maybe I was a bit naïve but those were my thoughts. Then I thought, Well, hang on a minute, this could work for business also as a great advertising tool. We were trying to brand MRI over in the UK, and even though we were doing thousands of exhibitions over there I thought what better way to promote myself and MRI than to buy a football club. But obviously, little did I know!

It probably turned out to be the worst thing I could do for my business, in all fairness. Being a football chairman put me in the press and subsequently MRI in the press, but for all the wrong reasons, and made me an easy target for the media.

Whenever we had had complaints before, it would be kept controlled and dealt with in-house. But as soon as I bought a football club people could say, 'Right, I'm going to the press!' and the press would leap on it because they felt they had an angle, to tear into this real estate company because the owner had just bought a football club: 'He's plastered all over Sky News, so let's do it.' Looking back now I can see it was the worst thing business-wise that I could have done, and even to this day, even though many of my businesses have long since stopped operating or gone into liquidation, I am written about in a negative light and find myself a target for some of the media.

BUYING A FOOTBALL CLUB (THIRD TIME LUCKY)

Going back to that summer, I remember sitting around one afternoon with all my advisors, and I had one of my business associates over in England, called Xavier Wiggins, call me. Xavier is a massive football fan – a Wimbledon fanatic, funnily enough – and I've know him for a long time. Whenever MRI did marketing in England it would be Xavier's company we would use. Anyway, Xavier called and explained that AFC Wimbledon was a team who were in the Ryman League at that time, and they could be a possibility for my ownership. With their rise from the ashes, it was a fantastic fairytale and a great club with massive potential from top to bottom.

AFC Wimbledon at that time were, and still are, owned by the fans, but I was told that it may be a good option to meet with the club's chairman to discuss a possible takeover, and if talks went well, etc. then maybe they could put it to the fans for a vote. Xavier felt that with my input and resources, they could get into the League a lot faster than it would take them with their own resources.

I met with Eric Samuelson, who was the Chief Executive of the club, at an office premises in Richmond. The meeting was to be one of the worst of my life. This man was the complete opposite to me. I remember walking through the door and straight away he was looking me up and down and staring at my watch. I've never sat in a room with a man that stared at me with so much contempt. He was completely against everything to do with me. I never had a problem with him, but he definitely had a problem with me, for whatever reason. I think the bottom line was that he didn't want this deal to go through and I think it was only as a favour that Xavier had got this guy to come and meet me, because I had money and I could bring new options to the football club.

A few days prior to this meeting I had been shown around the ground they were using as well as being taken to other potential sites for a new ground. I had started to get very nostalgic about how good would it be to get a club like AFC Wimbledon with such a great historical story like they had, not to mention the recent injustice involving MK Dons, back into or near the top flight of football.

However, as soon as I met with Eric it became very apparent that for him it wasn't about getting to the Championship and aiming for the top, it was more about keeping the club in existence, taking his kids to the games and running a tight ship. I can't say he wasn't ambitious, but it was obvious that he just wanted a football club that continued in existence, and given what had happened to the previous Wimbledon I understood him and of course appreciated where he was coming from.

Maybe he can say he was vindicated, because look where AFC Wimbledon are now – they are in the middle of League Two, they run a tight ship, they're in no debt, they have great support and great attendances. So maybe it's a good thing that Darragh MacAnthony didn't buy AFC Wimbledon, or maybe it's just fate that this wonderful story would run its natural course and the club end up near the top again. I hope so, anyhow, and always look for their results come match days.

However, I'm not the kind of guy to let that sort of thing affect me: I get up and move on. I then heard word of a chairman that had had enough of supporting his football club financially. It so happened that I was in the middle of buying a home in Berkshire and this other club I was looking at wasn't too far away. I remember going in and doing a deal pretty quickly on the basis of, I will own the football side and he will own the land. It's ironic now, I know, but that was the deal. This was in June and I was going away in July and wanted this deal completed before my return, ahead of the new season. I'm a man that wants everything yesterday and this was no different, as time was of course of the essence.

We signed a pre-reservation contract, where I put down £10,000 and paid half of the legal fees, etc. I then rented an island out in Ibiza and took Natalie and Calum away for ten days for a bit of relaxation ahead of this new, exciting period in my life. As always when I go away I like to take a few books. I'm a massive fan of sporting autobiographies, and I had three: David Gold's, of course, of Birmingham at the time but now at West Ham; a golfer's; and then I had Barry Fry's. So a bit of leisure reading was ahead of me, and little did I know that I would be meeting one of them in the flesh within weeks, and meeting the other on numerous occasions in years to come.

On the final day of my holiday I had a phone call from one of my advisors to tell me that the chairman of this football club had pulled out of the deal, due to him wanting to build a hotel on the land. He felt that with my takeover it would all be too complicated, so he gave back my ten thousand and said thank you but no thank you. It was a shame for this club and its fans, as it's since suffered a couple of relegations from the Blue Square Premier and it had decent potential.

That summer I arranged a private jet and accommodation for myself and some friends to go over to Germany to watch England play Portugal in the World Cup. I was really excited, as this would be my first World Cup, so I wanted to pull out all the stops. However, as I was on my way to the airport with Natalie, who was pregnant at the time, she began to get nasty pains in her stomach. So we made the decision not to board the jet and instead return home just in case this developed into something more serious. Everyone else went on the jet that I paid for, stayed in a lovely hotel, and watched the match. This cost me £80,000... Fortunately everything was fine with Natalie, it turned out to be some indigestion. So all my mates were there and I was watching it on TV, when I got a call from one of the boys saying, 'You'll never guess who I just met? Barry Fry, the owner of Peterborough United,' just to rub salt in the wounds. My pal was actually a die-hard Cambridge United supporter, so loved the opportunity to give Baz a bit of stick.

I was disappointed from my previous tries at trying to buy a club, but confident the right club would come about. Then one afternoon I had a phone call from Xavier telling me that he had bumped into Barry Fry and that he was saying he needed money and he needed to sell Peterborough United. Xavier told him that he might have someone in mind, to which Barry replied, 'Tell him to ring me in the morning!'

That night, when I returned home from work, my dad, who was over visiting from the States, shouted out from the living room: 'My God, you're so lucky you haven't bought this football club. You have to watch this show on TV. It's the most ridiculous thing you've ever seen in your life.' And there on the TV was *Big Ron Football Manager*, a new reality-show programme looking at the ins and outs of a football club, this one being Peterborough United.

I got on the phone to my guys in England and said, 'Get in touch with Barry Fry and find out what the crack is.' It was all very coincidental, how everything recently was Barry this, Barry that. Everywhere I looked or went there was something to do with Barry Fry. All very strange when you think about it. Posh fans will probably think Barry set it all up after reading this book!

Anyway, I watched the whole series of *Big Ron* and in the meantime my contacts in the UK were organising a meeting for me at Posh with Bob Symns, the Chief Exec, and Barry Fry, the owner. I took MJ who was my Number 2 at the time out there with me, and we stayed at the Dorchester Hotel in London. The minute I walked into Peterborough United and sat down with Barry in the boardroom, he was on at me about how he had had twenty people wanting to buy the club before me, but they were only really interested in the property and not the football. The fact that I was a property developer didn't settle Barry's nerves but I made it very clear from the start that my main focus was the football and I didn't give a toss about the land and developing it for homes.

As it turned out, myself and Barry ended up sitting for ages talking football, football, football, which convinced him of my real intentions, not to mention the fact that he was shocked by my knowledge of the game itself. Like a top salesman Barry took me to the 'show flat', which sealed the deal!

We went through the tunnel and out onto the pitch, and I couldn't believe how nice the ground was! OK, it's not Wembley, but for that level it was a great stadium, and I knew at that point that I had to have this football club by hook or by crook!

We went back into the boardroom to discuss the deal. Barry told me what he wanted, which was basically two loans, which he and another director, Alf Hand, had put into the club, to be paid off in full, which came to around £700k in total, and to take over the club's overdraft, which was then at £500k. I told Barry that I would be following this meeting up with an offer and went back to Spain for a few days to make him sweat. I like playing hardball, that's what I do, and to be fair, I could smell a bargain in the air, or so I thought.

A few days passed, and I emailed an offer to Bob for Barry to consider, which entailed paying half of the loans – £350,000 – meaning he would have to write off the rest, and of course I would meet the overdraft request in full.

Remember, I had listened to and watched for weeks on TV Barry moaning about having no money, so of course I smelt blood in the water and felt that he would snap my hand off with this offer... But of course, this is Barry we are talking about, and a reply came back pretty sharpish asking if it was April Fools' Day. I nearly fell off my chair, and then had to remember that this was football and not the real estate industry. I had to start getting used to a whole new world that was opening up in front of me and stop being surprised at this and surprised at that. Football is a different breed altogether.

I took a few days to digest that response and considered looking at other clubs but of course me being the impulsive person that I am meant that Peterborough United was going to be mine one way or another even if it meant shoving that April Fools' Day response up Barry's derriere.

I then decided that I would take Natalie over to watch a game. Darlington were coming over to London Road on 9th September so it was an opportunity to see The Posh live and take in the atmosphere of a home match, not to mention negotiate a little bit more if necessary.

Upon arriving at London Road, Barry took Natalie and myself into his office where we met Kirstine, Barry's wife, for the first time. I sat there as she began to give me the third degree, so to speak, telling me this was a family club and she hoped my intentions were right, etc. This slightly got my back up a bit, being the type of character that I am, but in her defence she was probably apprehensive about what would happen to Barry and to the staff that worked at the club, some of whom had been there for a lifetime. She was coming from the right place, and she interrogated me for about twenty minutes, but after I explained that I was in it for the football and not for profit and had no intention of firing people left, right and centre, she eased off and began to relax.

I remember sitting there in the directors' box, in the seat I sit in to this day. Nobody knew I was there, the fans certainly didn't know who I was, but I loved every minute of it – the atmosphere, the surroundings, the buzz... I was completely hooked. We lost 3-1 that afternoon, and I thought our team looked awful from top to bottom, never mind the style of football we were trying to play, but that had no bearing on my emotions at that moment in time.

After the match, I had some more discussions with Barry and it became very apparent that he wasn't going to budge from his asking price, not a penny. So I looked deeper into the finances surrounding the football club and then found the mess that was the holdings company and their controlling shareholder CH. Not only did this guy own the ground, but he also had the final say so in Barry selling his shares in the club. This was going to get messy, testing, and more than anything, complicated!

A COMPLICATED DEAL

Buying Peterborough United had gone from paying a few quid to a couple of directors to suddenly becoming a very complicated deal. It had become apparent that I wasn't going to be able to take over this football club without the permission of CH, a guy I didn't even know. I had heard that he was one of Barry's friends and that he (apparently) saved the club from going into administration and a few other things.

It seemed CH had bought the club from the previous regime for some unknown amount and then sold the football side to Barry for £1 and ended up owning the ground. So you had these two completely different companies, under one master company. Barry had all the shares for the football company and CH had all the shares for the company that owned the ground.

The deal was brilliant for a business person or an opportunist: buy a piece of land for a great price, get rid it of its biggest liability, which was the football club itself, and allow the football club to rent the ground back for £1 per annum. Barry took over a club that constantly lost money and CH owned the stadium, which could only ever appreciate in value in years to come. If the football club ever went belly up, then CH could sell the land and make a massive return on his investment. Let me be clear on this, CH did what 99% of property developers would do in his shoes and it was in no way illegal, but of course at risk was the future of a football club with years of history.

Me arriving on the scene was probably the last thing CH wanted, even though it probably allowed him to make a £7 million profit in the not too distant future. Had Barry stayed owner of the club, who knows what the outcome would have been.

Barry had gone to CH, all enthusiastic, telling him that this guy with loads of money wanted to buy the football club for all the right reasons and how he wants to do this and that, etc., and straight away CH was offish with Barry. It was like someone had just pissed on his parade. He didn't like the fact that Barry had this new guy who was all enthusiastic about the football – I think he liked having Barry in his own spot and felt that me coming along was stepping on his toes. Of course me being a well-known property developer didn't help my cause with CH either. So straight away this wasn't helping me in my quest to become owner of the Posh.

My next move, in fact the only move I could make, was to arrange to meet CH. I agreed a deal with Barry that I would buy the club for his asking price subject to obviously all of this shit coming good.

I had arranged some top lawyers in the UK to look over all the paperwork and investigate everything with a fine-tooth comb, the Peterborough United Holdings contract, the Peterborough United Football Club contract, etc., and to ensure all due diligence was done thoroughly.

In the meantime, we were always trying to look at ways to get round certain things and to bring me in as owner quicker than what looked to be the likely case.

In September Barry phoned me one day, out in Spain, and said, 'Listen, we have a League Cup game coming up against Premiership opposition Everton at London Road. Why don't you come along and we'll announce you as chairman? Get all the press involved, for a big press conference ahead of the match, and we'll tell everyone you have bought the club and you're the new Chairman.'

It was a bit hasty, in all fairness, because I hadn't actually done the deal yet, but Barry had worked me out by then and was pulling at my heart strings with the idea of the press conference, the Everton game, the fact it was a televised match – it all added to that sense of euphoria. So of course I agreed. Natalie couldn't come over at that point, as she was almost ready to drop with our second child, so my sister, my brother-in-law and some friends all came down and we stayed at the Haycock Hotel in Wansford. There was a big posse of us. This was going to be a big day, and an enjoyable one at that!

I did the press conference and felt that I had come across quite well. My manner was positive, because I'm a big believer that if you run a successful business you have to be positive. The Darragh MacAnthony ethos is to believe and achieve. My ambition for this club was to get it to the Premiership, and I meant every word and still do to this very day. I said that in seven years I wanted this football club to be in the Premier League, and at the time I felt invincible. I was making money like it was going out of fashion, my business was expanding quicker than I had ever imagined – too quickly in all honestly – I was going through a great spurt in my life and I felt I had grabbed the baton and was running at speed with it.

I knew that to do this I needed a plan. I couldn't just splash money at it constantly, and bring in £20,000-a-week players – that wasn't going to work, and that's not how I work. I needed to go back to the world of business and devise a plan top to bottom on how to achieve success with my new hobby.

I told the press that the first goal was to get out of League Two as quickly as possible, yesterday in fact, and I wanted trophies. Some people laughed at my ambitions but my outlook has always been reach for the stars and sometimes if you get close then that's good enough, but if you don't aim then what's the point?

Call me a dreamer, a fantasist, delusional and so on, but that's my outlook on life and it will never change. Why aim for mediocre when you can aim for exceptional?

After the press conference I took a walk into the city centre and went for a coffee, and whilst sitting there I received a phone call from Natalie. She told me, 'You're all over Sky News, and the fans are all giving their views on the move.' 'Lovely,' I said, and she continued, 'One woman is laughing at you, saying you have no chance of making a success of this football club.' I said, 'Baby, calm down, you're always going to have cynics and doubters, that's just life, but you know me, you know I get what I want one way or another.'

She wasn't used to seeing me get slagged off on TV, and I said, 'Get used to it, because worse is going to come whether we like it or not. I have put my head up over the pit to be shot down, and that's what usually happens if you become newsworthy.'

I remember when I started my first business and people laughed at me when I said I wanted eighty offices in twenty countries, but I did it. They don't have to believe what I say, *I* have to believe what I say, and that's what matters in one's quest to match beliefs with achievements.

On returning to London Road, I met with the manager, Keith Alexander. Keith was a lovely man, a very mild-mannered person. He chose to wear tracksuits to matches, which is something that I'm actually not a fan of, as I like managers to look the part in a suit. But he came in, with his tracksuit and cap on, and lounged in the chair all chilled and relaxed – nothing seemed to faze Keith. He was one of those guys who was pretty unflappable, and I quite like that in a person. I got a nice feel from Keith. To be honest, he was a difficult character not to like.

But with Keith being so relaxed, the two of us were like chalk and cheese, because everyone who knows me knows that I want things done yesterday. I said to Keith, 'Look, I want the club to win this League and get up into League One, and I'll give you X amount to spend and we can do this, and do that' and Keith said, 'Yeah, don't worry, it will happen, it's cool, it will be fine' – he was just so laid back.

Trying to get Keith to agree to spend money on the squad was proving to be difficult. It's like someone owning a car that's six years old and then someone offers to upgrade it to a brand new model with all the bells and whistles, but they turn the offer down as they are happy with model they have, even if it does have a hundred thousand miles on the clock.

You have to remember that Keith took the job knowing it was a low-budget role with the goals set of: 'Try your best to get into the play-off positions, you know, no pressure, if it happens, it happens.' He did it four times with Lincoln on a shoestring budget, his record was excellent, and now here I was demanding silverware instantly.

With kick-off time approaching, I stepped out onto the pitch, where I was introduced to the fans. They gave me a great reception, and then I was presented with a picture of the stadium by Brian Mawhinney, who is a local MP and at the time was Chairman of the Football League.

The atmosphere was electric: nearly 11,000 people were there that night with the match also being screened live on Sky Sports.

We went 1-0 down in the first half by an own goal from Jude Sterling, but when Trevor Benjamin scored our equaliser in the 56th minute to bring it back to 1-1 I had never felt a feeling like it, it was incredible. Sadly Everton went on to score a winner in the 87th minute when Gary Cahill bundled it into our net. But loss aside, we really gave those Prem boys a game, and I just wanted more and more of it, I loved every second. And from that moment on, all I wanted was success for the mighty Posh.

That day that we went public with my takeover, Posh were sitting in tenth place in League Two with 14 points on the board after nine games played.

I sat with Keith in November that year and said, 'Right, what do we need?' To which Keith replied, 'I don't understand, what do you mean what do we need?' 'To get out of this League, what do we need, player-wise, to succeed?' I said.

The guy looked at me like I had two heads. 'Ah, we're fine, the squad's all fine,' he said. 'The squad's not fine, it was fine before I came, but now I want the squad to be exceptional,' I said.

In fairness to Keith he hadn't really had that before, he had always been used to working on such a tight budget, and in I came offering him anything he liked. He obviously wasn't used to that sort of conversation. The previous week he had had Barry saying, 'Look, try and aim for a playoff spot if you can' and this week he had me saying, 'We need to win the League.' It was a massive change in circumstances for him.

Remember Keith wasn't my manager, Barry hired him, and Barry understood that. He said from the very start, 'Look, if you want to change Keith then that's fine, because he was not your appointment,' to which I said, 'Look, I don't wanna fire Keith, because he hasn't done anything wrong.' They had beaten Ipswich in the cup and nearly pulled off a shock against Everton in the cup. League results were a bit up and down, but we were seventh in the League at that stage so there was no cause for panic on my part.

I went back to Spain and sat down to draw up a firm plan of exactly what I wanted from Posh and where I wanted the club to go for the next seven years. To get a team to the Premier League you need something like a £100 million, and although I had amassed a decent chunk of change by then, it wasn't quite that much. So I had to look at how we could do things in a clever way, without having to be silly.

I also had to get over this big issue with paperwork, and work out how I could complete the takeover legally. So I arranged a meeting with CH. I flew back to England and met CH at the Dorchester. This meeting was to last five hours: there was me, KC, who was a director at the club at the time working essentially for CH, and I had my Number 2, MJ, with me.

It was apparent in the first ten minutes of that meeting that CH and I were never going to get on. He had an ego, I had an ego, and I think he felt I was this young whippersnapper coming in and pissing on his parade. The guy talks a million miles an hour and is obviously a great salesman, but straight away the pair of us didn't get on.

Barry came along half way through, but didn't stay long. It was obvious that CH didn't want Barry in the room and apparent that CH had a real issue with him as the conversation turned more onto Barry this and Barry that, rather than focusing on the football club.

If the truth be told – and Posh fans won't want to hear this – if I had agreed to fire Barry Fry from his job at Posh, then I have no doubt CH would have approved the deal in a heartbeat. I felt at this stage that this wasn't really about me, it was more about Barry. But I've never been one to take an easy option and I'm loyal to the core, so I wouldn't entertain this. I made it clear that Barry shouldn't be of concern anymore to CH.

Instead, I made it clear to CH that we were there to talk about my purchase of the football club and the ground, so I said 'Look, what do you want for it?' 'Twelve million,' he replied.

I said, 'Look, I ain't giving you £12 million for the ground,' to which he said, 'Well OK, what are you going to offer me for the ground?' I said,

'I can probably get to £8 million,' which he turned down straight away. I said, 'CH, the ground isn't worth £12 million, you didn't pay anywhere near that' and so it got pretty heated. In fact it wasn't even worth £8 million, but in my mind paying over the top for it might lead to fewer issues and less stress.

'Well then, you can't come in, and any monies you've given to Barry need to come to me,' he said. 'The football side is nothing to do with you,' I replied, to which he said, 'Well, I can stop all this happening and stop you coming in.'

It all got very aggressive, and at this stage my back was up, and I had had enough of CH.

Over the coming weeks I had some more meetings, but this time via KC. He was trying to play the peacemaker and get CH everything he needed, rather than looking after mine or the club's best interests. A big problem I think was that when Barry owned the football club he only had to pay £1 in rent every year, but by me taking over he would have to start paying £78,000 a year. It all became clear that they wanted me to sign a new lease with them, and that if I signed a new lease they would let the deal happen but I would have to pay a lot more than £78,000 a year. So it was all about money. CH would tell you right now that that's what it was all about, he had no interest in me, and no interest in the football club, it was just money. The end goal for CH was to have me sign a new lease with an end date of 2014 or 2015 which meant quite possibly the football club having to find a new home after that.

Keep in mind that CH only paid six figures for the ground and he wanted a return on his investment of over £11 million, which was never going to happen in a million years. He knew that I was excited about buying a club and he wanted to exploit that and use me to get things he couldn't possibly get with Barry still owning the club. So me coming in had actually turned into another opportunity for CH.

Don't get me wrong, I hold no ill feelings towards the previous regime and at the end of the day he did what he had to do, and I am sure 99.9% of people would have done exactly the same thing. Buy a property dirt-cheap and sell it for as much as you can. CH is a big player and knows an opportunity when he sees one.

At this point everyone around me was telling me to walk away – my dad, my friends, everyone. At the end of the day I wanted to buy a football club as a whole, the team, the ground, the lot, and I certainly didn't foresee all the shit that was to follow. My advisors were telling me, 'This is crazy, you're being held to ransom, you're going to put all this money into a club that has no assets', but me being me, I was in love. I was immersed. Whether it was my ego or my naivety, I don't know, but at the end of the day, as most football fans will understand, I followed my heart instead of my head, which, considering I'm a business man, was a rarity and in fact pretty naive.

So I spoke with Barry and I said, 'Right, for this deal to go through and for you to have your money and me to put money into this club, you're going to need to give me Power of Attorney.' This was basically a contract to be put in place where Barry, as the owner, would give over the club's Power of Attorney to me. This would give me full and sole access on all decisions which were to be made on the club, and this was something CH could do nothing about legally. So I commissioned my lawyers to draw the document up sharpish, and we signed it. From that point onwards, any say to do with the football club would come through me. This protected myself and the money I had invested in the club, as at any time I could sell assets and get my money back if the worst case scenario happened and I could never complete the purchase

In the meantime I was still fighting to gain full ownership, and this dragged on and on, to the point where it wasn't completed until the following September 2007. It felt like I was telling the fans 'It will happen soon' a million times and it was getting frustrating for everyone. We eventually found a loophole where I could buy Barry's shares without even having to consult CH.

We basically found a grey area and went for it, but of course we knew that CH would go fucking ape shit and throw his lawyers at us to try to stop this from happening. CH began throwing all sorts of threats my way, saying that he was going to send in the receivers to wind up the club, that he was going to do this, and do that... But it was all poker face, and I'm very good at poker! At this point I had been in this situation for ten months and was in for well over a million pounds spent on the football club, so this was a battle I was never going to lose.

It turned out that CH wanted a new lease signed. The current one was going to run for a long time and he wanted to put in a lease that had an end date on it, say 2015/16, with the overall aim I expect that when it came to that deadline we would be out on our ear and he would have his land back. But up our sleeves was the covenant that the council had in place on the ground, and without the council lifting this covenant he could never sell the ground, so it would be worthless to him.

So I said, 'Right, let's get an independent audit in to value the ground and we can talk about the possibility of a new lease.' Then this guy came in who didn't really listen to what we had to say and valued the ground at £280,000 a year, so we had gone from paying £1 a year,, to £78,000 a year, to £280,000 a year. I say independent but it was one of three assessors that were chosen by our current landlord to come up with this yearly rental value.

We met with CH's lawyers, and these guys rubbed me up the wrong way from the start.

We were in this big boardroom, where CH began to wind me up big time about a recently aired BBC documentary that had portrayed me in a bad light business-wise, after which the pair of us nearly ended up in fisticuffs across the table. I said to him, 'You are fuck-all to me, you mean nothing to me, you're nothing but a thug, and if you want to take this outside the good old fashioned way, lead the way.' At which point the lawyers stepped in, but that's how heated these discussions were at that time. Many people I'm sure would have been intimidated with these tactics, but that was his way of trying to get what he wanted. For some that sort of approach may have worked, but it wasn't going to be working with me. No fucking way. I couldn't give a fuck what he had or where it had come from. At the end of the day, if you want to go one on one with me then that's a battle I will quite happily take on.

I never did like bullies and in my mind he was a bully with a large bank account, end of story. Truth is CH was not a bully, but in fact a ruthless business man used to getting what he wants. Sounds familiar right?

His lawyer then started threatening to come after me over the deal that I had struck with Barry, so I said to my guys, 'Look, I just want this prick off my back. We'll sign a new lease for X amount of years, I'll pay the legal fees, etc., and then CH has to agree to give up any challenge on my ownership.'

It was such a hard decision, because on one hand, if I don't sign the lease I've got this guy who's going to drag me through the high courts, he's going to jeopardize my ownership, and on the other hand, I sign a new lease and risk the football club not having a home come 2015. So it was an incredibly difficult decision to make but I had to choose one, and I chose the latter.

In the end I was able to complete my takeover in full where £1 was exchanged with Barry Fry and the rest, as they say, is history.

MY PERSONAL SITUATION

At the time when I took over Posh, *The Times'* Rich List had me at a ridiculously high position with something like £150 million. I think they based that on the value of MRI with the company turning over around £100 million a year, and from that I imagine the company would be worth around that figure if not more.

Through many various business activities, I earnt a lot, but then with my lifestyle I spent a lot also. I was never a great saver, never have been, and so yes, I've had millions and millions of pounds but then I've also spent millions and millions of pounds. Look at the club, for instance: to this date I have put over £10 million into it. I've never been shy of spending money, or speculating to accumulate.

As I built my various businesses in the early days, my rule of thumb was always to spend as much on building the business as was coming into the business income wise. The first five years of MRI, for example, was month to month, making payroll and covering bills as we continually expanded into new regions and employed more and more staff.

Growing up in my twenties I lived the ultimate lifestyle, the kind of lifestyle I'm sure everyone would love to have. I bought the best cars, the biggest homes, travelled on private jets, had the best holidays, and I had the ultimate hobby – owning a football club. Maybe I was naïve, but remember I had worked very hard to get to that point and I wasn't going to not enjoy myself.

At the back end of 1999 I had been sacked from a real-estate company for not being robotic enough for them – I was too strong willed and self motivated. So in 2000 I dusted myself down and set out alone with £4,000 in my pocket. I took a lot of big risks at the start that thankfully they paid off, not to mention working night and day to be successful.

In the space of six years my business grew from doing one deal a month to a thousand a month. Real estate in Spain, especially at that time, just exploded, and when others were opening up in one country I was opening up in five countries at once. Every penny I made went straight back into the business to expand, and there was a three or four year period where we were making a prolific amount of money, but also spending a prolific amount of money.

Unfortunately when you're making a lot the chances are you're spending a lot, the overall wage bill, the commissions etc etc.

On our marketing side we were spending millions of euros each year. So we were spending a lot of money – could I have spent a lot less and saved a lot more? Yes, absolutely, but I was young and got caught up in the success in my twenties.

When the world took a turn for the worse, on the other hand, my business went down the tube, probably to a lot of people's liking. When the world is in a recession no one wants to buy overseas real estate any more, and at that time I lost 85% of my wealth in an instant, gone.

A lot of my businesses went insolvent and into liquidation, and a lot of people owed me money. I was owed €14 million from developers and then another €22 million from clients on apartments I had built for them but then they couldn't complete on, due to the world financial crisis.

I lost a lot of wealth in the Madoff Ponzi scandal as well, which didn't help. Sometimes when bad news starts, its tough to stick the brakes on and stop it. I have no doubt there are millions of people around the world who ended up in the same or a similar position to myself. That's life, I am afraid, and 'what doesn't kill you makes you stronger' is my response.

So I went from being worth over £100 million and with the idea of spending £500k a year on a football club without fluttering an eyelash, to suddenly finding it pretty hard to find the small fortune needed to be invested into the football club each year, and all in the space of around two and a half years, but I did it, because I loved my club and luckily the plans I had put together for the Posh helped, because it paid for itself, so to speak.

My ambitions were to be cash rich, with around £100 million, and then stop working, but I'm nowhere near that figure. At my peak I was on course, but to every success story there is a dip, and I have been in a dip for a little while. But everyone loves a fight back and that's what I intend to do.

Remember that with this wealth comes a lot of negativity. I've had some pretty harsh and nasty stuff written about me over the years and unfortunately it's true what people say, when you put your head above the pit and you get to the top rung, you're setting yourself up to be shot at. But I don't let it bring me down. I never went into business expecting to be loved and to be popular, I went into business wanting to make money and become successful in order to provide for myself and my family, which, thank God, I have achieved. I also went into business hoping to leave a legacy for my children and to have them take it over in the future. Had the recession not happened, I can comfortably state that my business would be around today and one of the largest in the world.

IDEOLOGY

I remember sitting in my office, just after the Everton game, and looking through all the figures and paperwork, etc. I looked through the squad list and the youth players we had, and the only player that had made it into the pro set up at that time was Jamie Day. For me, that needed to change.

I looked at the wage bill, the ages of players, where they had played before, the money going out, the money coming in.

Obviously our income was poor, our attendances were shocking, and there was no feel-good factor with the club. That needed to change. I needed to make the city of Peterborough fall in love with their football club again; I had to bring excitement back to London Road. I needed the city to realise that we were ambitious. No longer would we be settling for crowds of 2,500 or 3,500; no longer would we be aiming for a play-off spot in League Two if we were lucky; and no longer were we looking to buy players like your Trevor Benjamins or Danny Crows of this world (no disrespect to them).

We were going to be a new football club: young, hungry and dynamic. We were going to have a new policy of creating exciting football, and to do that we needed a young ambitious team that scored lots of goals and played attractive football whilst being led by a young ambitious manager who wanted to achieve. We needed the media to get on top of this, to get people to sit up and notice of us so that at the least our own home city would do all that they could to attend our matches.

So I thought, Right, how can we do this? I can't change the manager, the guy's done nothing wrong, so I will give him a fair crack, and if he can buy into what we are doing then fine, but if he can't, then I am going to have to address the situation.

I began writing up a list of players I felt would suit the football club: Izale McLeod from MK Dons for £1 million was the most expensive player I suggested, and I remember taking that name to the manager, Keith, and he nearly fell off his chair, '£1 million for a striker?' He had never been offered that kind of money before and I'm not so sure it sat right with him.

I still remember the joy on Barry's face as he made the call to Pete Winkleman at MK Dons to offer that kind of money for one player. In fairness to Pete he turned the bid down and looking back it was probably the best thing that could have happened. If you look back at past events, Posh spending a million quid on a player could and probably would have had disastrous consequences on and off the field.

I looked at our current squad to see who out of the lot we could keep. Jamie Day and possibly Adam Newton were the only two I could think of having a future at Peterborough United, if our ambitions of back-to-back promotions were to be fulfilled. We needed players who could not just play at League Two level, but who could grow, improve, play at higher levels and have a serious asset value to the club.

Our squad consisted of the likes of Simon Yeo, Jude Sterling, Chris Plummer, Ryan Semple, Luke McShane, Paul Carden and David Farrell. Now David, I know, was and still is a massive legend for the club, but age was catching up with him at that point. I mean the average age of our squad at that point was around thirty, and I knew that with this we had no resale opportunities from the players and no way of making money to regenerate back into the team.

Posh were an average run-of-the-mill typical League Two club hoping to get lucky and squeak into a play-off position with a pipeline dream of promotion into League One. Obviously with this they would then look to spend the following season fighting relegation. A harsh but true reflection of the football club when I first walked in the door.

I thought long and hard on this, and then suddenly thought, well, hang on, why don't we look to the League below, non-League, and pick the best players from each position. For instance, if you picked eleven of the best footballers from the twenty-odd teams in that League you would create one hell of a team capable of getting out of League Two.

But with that would come conditions: They had to be between eighteen and twenty-three, they had to be young enough to improve. They also had to be a large mix of ex-Football League players, kids that began their careers at Football League clubs but were unable to make the final cut, like George Boyd, who had come from Charlton, McLean from Leyton Orient and so on and so on.

On each contract offered to a player they had to live within fifteen miles of the ground, preferably in the same street, because I wanted a bunch of eighteen- to nineteen-year-old kids living together, growing up together and jelling as a team, as a unit. It would create an unflappable team spirit on and off the field.

I wanted excitement and flair, and most of all I wanted two pacy strikers who were both capable of scoring twenty goals plus a season. I was never into the 'one big man one small man' prophecy: I liked pace, flair, and the ability to score a shitload of goals.

So we went with this policy. I hadn't quite refined it as much as I would have liked, but we went out there looking for the best eleven. As I was in the middle of looking at this, Barry called me to say that Keith had contacted him in regards to some targets, Josh Low, who was a 28-year-old winger from Leicester City and Micah Hyde, a 33-year-old centre midfielder from Burnley.

I strangely agreed to this because I felt it would boost the fans and the club as a whole. Micah was on £4,000 a week with a three-year deal and Josh was on £3,000 a week on a four-and-a-half year deal in League Two. It was mega money for Peterborough United and for League Two but we felt that those two signings would be perfect to blend in with youth we were trying to bring through the doors.

Don't get me wrong, these were great players for this level, Micah especially because he was playing top-flight football with Watford a few seasons before, a club where he went on to play over 250 times. He was going to be our captain, which was a massive part of the upcoming jigsaw we were about to put together.

For the plan to work, I knew I would need to add one or two experienced players to help those young players along, but I knew there would come a point where we no longer looked for players over the age of twenty-eight: it just wasn't feasible for the bigger picture and didn't fit my ideology or the long-term policy for the club.

If you look at the players we have now, for instance, five years on, the ones that have grown will go on and make this club a lot of money. Look at Craig, for instance, that one alone justifies everything. Yes, we paid over £100,000 for Scott Rendell and yes, we paid £150,000 for Liam Hatch – but remember they were on really basic wages and when they were loaned out we got all that money back and eventually more. The reason we now have players valued at millions of pounds is because of the plan I created, and because the gaffer bought into it and made it all come to fruition.

NON-LEAGUE FOOTBALL

I used to subscribe to the non-League paper, and I would trawl through this every week and pick players that were playing well and getting rave reviews, and I would then sign up to all these club's message boards on the internet to find out the reactions from the fans. Whether you like it or not, that's where you find out if the player is talented, good or bad, because they are seeing these guys play week in, week out and would have a non-biased honest opinion, whether it was controversial or not.

So I knew Aaron McLean was the top goal scorer in the League at that time; Craig Mackail-Smith was up there; and whenever Dagenham and Redbridge were mentioned, along with Craig's name was always Shane Blackett – the guy was always in the Team of the Week section. With Aaron I knew all about his history with Aldershot and Leyton Orient, I had seen video of a lot of his goals, I knew he was an exciting talent and would give us pace, and after reading about Craig's performances and style of play, I remember dreaming of these two causing havoc with League Two and League One defences and leading our assault as we climbed the Football League ladder.

I remember also going onto the Stevenage Borough message forum under a made-up name, saying I was a scout looking for talent, and a fan ended up sending me a link to some online footage of a player they called 'The White Pele', George Boyd. When I watched the footage on my computer that day I sat bolt upright and took notice, as all these magnificent goals were finding the net from this skilful young lad. It wasn't only his goals, it was his technical skill, flair and ability that got me so excited, and all I could think was, Why is this youngster playing in non-League? Has the football world gone mad, is it full of poor scouts, or are the League clubs too snobbish?

I came over to England and contacted Barry and said, 'Right, I want you to sign Craig Mackail-Smith, Aaron McLean, Shane Blackett and most importantly George Boyd!'

Barry said, 'Well, we all know about George Boyd, but he's got a £260,000 payout on his contract, loads of clubs have been in for him but won't pay the price tag and feel that his lack of pace will stop him playing at the top level.' 'The lads only nineteen, I couldn't give a fuck about the price, do the deal,' I said. 'But this is how you do the deal,' I said. 'Do the deal on a never-never basis' 'What do you mean never-never?' he said. 'Well, if George is going to cost £260,000, do the deal, but do it over two years, 50k now, 50k next year, and add-ons here and there. Do the deal but don't do it in one big lump, put it on the drip,' I said.

Aaron McLean was the same: he cost us £100k which we paid over ten months. Mackail- Smith and Blackett cost us £250k which we paid over twenty-four months. This helped us financially and didn't kill us by breaking the bank. It was prudent buying for us whilst in League Two and it wouldn't stick a noose around our necks whilst doing it.

Barry spoke with Keith about my requests, and it was clear Keith didn't really want all of these players, bar Aaron, but I'll be honest, he didn't really have a choice in the matter.

In fairness to Keith, he knew non-League really well, and knew all about Aaron, George and Craig. He definitely wanted Aaron: before I had even come to the club he had Aaron down as a player he wanted to bring in. In fact the irony was that if you wanted to buy the best non-League talent in Britain, Keith Alexander was your man. However, results were OK and Keith just wasn't buying into the fact that our club needed a complete overhaul from top to bottom.

He didn't want George, because we had Peter Gain on the left at the time, who was regarded as our most skilful player, and Keith felt he preferred Peter over George.

I went down to the club and spoke with Keith personally and told him I was going to do a deal for George. Keith's opinion was: 'Chairman, we don't need him, I don't want him, Peter Gain is just as good,' to which I said, 'Well look, I want to buy the best non-League talent out there, and George is in that bracket,' and to be fair I couldn't see Peter Gain ever earning us seven figures in the years to come.

I remember Aaron coming down with his agent; I sat and did the deal myself. He had been on his way to Wolves and luckily Barry had managed to persuade him to drop into London Road on his way.

His agent was a right wide boy and tried to close the deal down straight away. Aaron, on the other hand, was a lovely guy, and said that he wanted until 9 o'clock that evening to think about it so he could speak with his girlfriend. So I gave him till that point to let us know or else we would not be going through with the deal. Nine o'clock came, and no phone call from Aaron, and I remember the next morning walking through the cathedral in Peterborough when my mobile rang, and it was Aaron saying, 'I'm in my car, I'm on my way up.' I said, 'Turn around and go back, we're not signing ya.' Then there was a silence and then eventually, 'What?' To which I said, 'Look, I told you, you had until 9 o'clock last night to sign and you didn't.' Maybe I was going soft but in the end I said 'OK, look, you've called me personally, we'll sign you. Now get your arse over to Peterborough.'

This may seem harsh or strange but I am a firm believer that if somebody leaves the boardroom, the likelihood of closing that deal diminishes by the hour. I guess I was adopting my business techniques to football. Rightly or wrongly, I felt it was the right way to do things.

These young lads were of course calculated risks, but remember they weren't on big money at that stage, we're talking £800 a week, £1300 with bonuses, etc. We were offering them a platform, a stage to perform and earn the big move with big dough following.

They were all given four-year contracts, along with my word that if the club progressed and if they improved as individuals then I would reward them by offering them new deals.

People laughed at the time about four-year deals, but that was our protection as a club. If you sign a shit-hot talent and stick him on a four-year deal, you're protected; if you sign him, give him a two-year deal, then that season he scores thirty goals, you're fucked.

I remember when we were sat down doing the Aaron deal, Aaron's agent said, 'Look, I have another player you may be interested in, Michael Knightly. Do you know him?' And in fact I knew all about him, he could play wide right, left, he had fifteen goals already under his belt, a good player. 'He's Aaron's best mate, and you can have him for £25,000,' he said. 'Go get him on the phone and get him down here,' I said.

Keith was in on that meeting and he said, 'Look chairman, I know you're bringing Aaron in, Craig in, George in, and I have no room for Michael Knightly in the squad, plus I've seen him play a few times and I'm not overly keen on him'.

So at that point, because I had pushed all these other players on him I felt kind of guilty, so I let this one go. Of course, he went on to sign for Wolves and was banging them in, and if he hadn't have got injured would of gone for a lot of money.

Now, you're not always going to get them all right – for every Boydy there's a Kieran Charnock, for every Aaron there's a Danny Blanchett, and I knew that with this strategy we were going to take some hits. With every great player you were going to get a couple which wouldn't come off and cost us a small amount of money, but I knew that financially the good would outweigh the bad. As some examples of a few that we took a hit on: we spent £50,000 on Danny Mills and Romone McRae. We knew Danny had scored a few goals against Glasgow Rangers in a friendly, and we beat Rangers to his signature. Romone was a player who had raw ability and we thought we could develop him into a good player, but sadly both signings didn't pay off.

We spent £5,000 on Danny Blanchett, who was on Liverpool's radar (apparently). Kieran Charnock was a highly rated centre-back, and was in non-League's Team of the Year for that season. He cost us £50,000 and did OK at League Two level, but when we made the step up to League One it was apparent we needed someone better.

Then we had Shaun Batt, who cost us £5,000 at the time from Fisher Athletic and went on to make us £350,000 with his sale to Millwall. Paul Coutts we bought for £15,000 from the Highland Leagues and went on to make us £500,000 with his sale to Preston North End. Craig Morgan was a free transfer that earned the club nearly £400,000.

Striker-wise we tried Scott Rendell, Liam Hatch and Rene Howe. None of those players worked out, but remember their job was to dislodge the Mac attack, so that was no easy task. This led to many of them going out on loan, and in return their wages would be covered completely and through initial loan fees we would then recoup their initial fees that we paid originally.

Barry had always been a big fan of non-League football, but even he thought that my policy was a bit strong, that I shouldn't be swamping the team with it and that I should look to add some Football League experience to the blend. But overall he believed that what I was doing was right for the future of this football club. Still, it was going to be a work-in-progress and we had to bide our time.

THE HOLY TRINITY

So we captured Aaron McLean's signature, which was a massive achievement for us, and it paid off straight away. His pace, his ability shone through, and the fans took to him from the off. Both on the field and off he was different class.

The Boyd deal was a very smooth one. Phil Wallace from Stevenage was true to his word: if someone met the £260,000 fee asked for him then he would be allowed to leave. We paid the asking price on a drip basis and George was then given permission to speak with us.

In fairness it was the dream deal. His agent, Clive, is a top bloke and only wanted the best for George, and the four-year contract was signed there and then.

When I first met George he was a shy lad, who was working part-time in a shop to boost his wages. We sat together in the stands and spoke about his ambition and desire to do well in the game.

I remember going to a fans' forum whilst these talks with George were going on, and I told the fans that we were in talks with the best young winger in non-League. I wasn't giving any more away, but I was very excited about George Boyd signing for our football club. Little did people know that he would go on to be the highest-paid player in the club's history. and rightly so.

When people heard the price we had paid for George, I think it shocked a lot of people, not just our fans but bodies in the world of football. We had just completed a record signing for a player in non-League. If you look back now, George was effectively a free signing after the loan money received from Nottingham Forest later on in his career, but we didn't know that then.

I knew from the very start that Keith wasn't keen on playing him, and he didn't really come into his own until Darren came into the building. But this was something Keith had to get used to if he wanted to be manager of Darragh MacAnthony's Posh.

This isn't me picking the team, this is me as owner asking management to buy into my vision and policy for the football club.

Craig Mackail-Smith's deal was slightly different to the other two. We moved in for him in the November and put down a payment of £50,000 for him and Shane Blackett, with the agreement that both would join Peterborough United in January. That was the deal, both clubs were happy and the players were happy. Craig signed the deal and was happy with the wages agreed.

So basically what would happen then was that, come January, the players' registration paperwork would come over to us, and they would become players of Peterborough United.

Through the coming weeks we caught word of multiple clubs sniffing around Craig and unsettling him, which obviously we weren't happy about. So Barry got on the phone to Craig's agents (he had a tribe of them who weren't even officially registered), to ask what was going on. Then these two-bit idiots began saying they wanted more money, he didn't want to come to Posh anymore, and basically trying all they could to get out of our agreed deal. Barry rang me and said, 'He's not coming.' I said, 'What do you mean, he's not coming?' 'He's not coming, the manager (Darren Ferguson) has been down to meet him and he's told the manager he doesn't want to come,' Barry informed me. 'Barry, get in your fucking car and drive to his parents' house and get this sorted out.' I knew Craig's father was very influential in his career, so I said, 'Sit in front of his dad and tell him, if this boy doesn't turn up for training Monday morning, I'm going to sit him in the fucking stands for four-and-a-half years of his career! Why? Because I fucking can!' I demanded.

No player was ever going to hold my football club to ransom, and we had spent a lot of time and money on Craig. More to the point, he was a vital part of our jigsaw. Funnily enough, come Monday morning Craig turned up for training, and in fairness to the lad, once he got over that and put his head down he was an absolute pleasure to have on board.

But that's my way of managing, the no bullshit approach, and most of the time it was effective. Barry, the manager and everyone else had given up on Craig playing for Posh, but because of my determination and will to succeed, we created a true Posh legend that would go down in folklore, so it turned out to be a good bit of business!

I suppose the Holy Trinity, as they have become affectionately known, have been the symbol of my time as owner of the football club so far.

Just looking at their records, statistics and what they achieved in their time playing together cements their status as legends in the Posh history books. The Trinity also sent shivers down the spines of opposing managers and players alike throughout League One and League Two during our back-to-back success and our return to the championship recently.

MY FIRST BIG DECISION

When I first took over the football club, I felt Keith Alexander was completely under-rated. This guy's record spoke for itself.

In 2002/3 he steered Lincoln, who were two places from the bottom of the table at the time, to finish in a play-off position. He went on to take Lincoln into the play-offs for the next consecutive three seasons, giving him the unbelievable record of being the only manager to lead a team to four consecutive play-off defeats. And all this was achieved on a shoestring budget.

I remember this period like it was yesterday. If we go back to November 2006, I remember being at my home many miles away from the UK, and I would be sitting there on match days watching the results come in on Soccer Saturday. Some great results were coming through: we had five games that month in all competitions and won four of them. McLean was already scoring lots of goals, so things were going nicely to plan.

I got Keith a Number 2 at his request in the form of Tommy Taylor. Tommy came in to help out with the training, etc., and gave Keith another pair of hands.

Come December, I went off to Ireland for a few days and went to watch a George Michael concert. Fans will tell you the club usually suffered from the Posh Christmas Jinx at this time of year, but at this point the team had played three games, won two and drawn one, so all was looking good.

I flew over to the States on business and much to my horror our results took a turn for the worst. Chester at home, lost 2-0; Lincoln at home, lost 2-1; Barnet away, lost 1-0; and at this time I was panicking big time. I would speak with Barry at the end of each match and continuously ask, 'What the fuck is going on?' I couldn't understand how we were suddenly on such a poor run of form results wise.

Keith and I very rarely, if at all, spoke on the phone. Everything was done through Barry, and I only saw Keith when I was back in England. I had been saying to Barry for a few weeks that I wanted to change the manager, but he would always persuade me to give him more time. In fairness to Barry, Keith was the manager that he had employed so maybe he felt he needed to protect him, and maybe it was Barry's experience coming through, advising me so that I wasn't seen as the hatchet man.

But all this time I'm thinking about wanting to get my own manager in, a young ambitious manager that wants to work with the policies I have put in place. That was not trying to belittle Keith or knock Keith – remember, I didn't employ Keith. He wasn't my manager.

When January arrived I wanted to forget December had even happened and concentrate fully on this back-end to the season. I went away on holiday to the Bahamas for ten days and slumped back in my chair when on 1st January we lost 2-0 to Walsall at home, and drew 1-1 on 6th January at home to Plymouth in the FA Cup.

At this point I had had enough. This couldn't carry on at this pace. I had spent big money on the likes of Hyde, Low, Boyd and McLean, players more than capable of succeeding at this level. I spoke to Barry and said, 'Look, I'm going to give him one more chance, if we lose on Saturday against Darlington Keith's got to go.'

We lost that match 3-1 against Darlington and it was to be our sixth consecutive loss on the trot. Our attendances were shit and averaging around 4,000 and I had to sit back and dig deep into everything to look at the issues within the club. And boy, did we have issues.

Ground issues, ownership issues, fan issues, Barry Fry issues, media issues off the back of *Big Ron*. We had a reputation for playing a style of football at that time, and again that's no disrespect to Keith, but we had a very direct way of playing that wasn't the prettiest on the eye. Our great reputation of the past in creating great players like Matthew Etherington and Simon Davies had gone, and if you looked at our squad as assets, there were none that were screaming out to me. So all these problems needed solving, and on top of all that we didn't look like we would win another football match. My desire for bringing in my blueprint of a new manager was at the forefront of my mind.

My aim that year was to get straight out of League Two and at this point I felt that time was slipping away from us. I called Barry and said, 'Keith has to go!'

Barry arranged a meeting with Keith and in all fairness he took the decision really well. He was paid up in full and no ill words were spoken.

I had never had a single argument with Keith Alexander and I never had a problem with the man. After he left I don't think it was long before he was back in work, and further down the line, whenever he needed players to help him out, we would do our bit.

To this day Keith is the only manager that I have let go and felt guilty for doing so, and that was due to the fact that he was such a lovely guy and top manager. But the bottom line was, he wasn't my manager. Keith sadly passed away in March 2010, and I remember getting a phone call from the club telling me the sad news In the days following Keith's death I arranged for certain costs for his funeral to be paid, out of respect for such a top man in the world of football and for his service to Posh.

WELCOME DARREN FERGUSON

After Keith's dismissal, his Number 2, Tommy Taylor, took over for a few games and we continued the bad run of form: Plymouth away in the FA cup second leg, lost 2-1 and then Stockport at home lost 3-0.

Tommy was an experienced manager and had managed at international level with Grenada.

He had asked for the job permanently, but that was never going to happen. We once had a management meeting where he said to me, 'You are never going to get success with a bunch of non-League kids.' From that moment on, I had no time for Tommy, but during this interim period he was the only option we had.

I had a lot of business going on at that time, and I was out in the States working long hours. I called Barry and said, 'Right, we need a young, ambitious guy, someone who is maybe still playing football, preferably someone who has been captain of their club before, someone who has started their coaching badges and wants to succeed and be a top manager. But most of all this guy will need to buy into our ethos that we are trying to instill into Peterborough United.'

Some people saw this as a gamble, but for me this is what I did every day in business – I took young, inexperienced and hungry individuals and built them up into successful people, which in turn brought my business great success. So this was to be no different, for me this was the only route we were going to take.

One person I had in mind was Andy Ritchie, who was doing a great job at Barnsley at the time. He was young, was a former player, and I think won two promotions in his time, so he fitted the bill.

I remember Kenny Dalgleish made a call to Barry for his friend Bobby Williamson, a guy who had managed at Hibernian in Scotland and Plymouth Argyle previously.

A few names were coming to light; then one evening Barry called me and said, 'I have a name for ya, and I'm not sure how you're going to feel about it.' 'Who?' I said. 'Darren Ferguson.' 'Darren Ferguson? Isn't he with Wrexham still playing?' I said. 'Yeah he is, but he's thirty-four, he's just been turned down for the management job for them again, and his dad's been on the phone asking if we will give him a shot,' Barry said. I said 'OK, let me go and do some research on the guy and I'll get back to ya.'

I went away and looked at all the Wrexham message boards and it was apparent he was obviously very popular with their fans; he had captained the club; had started his coaching badges; and had, for the second time, been overlooked for the Wrexham job. Barry contacted Wrexham to find out a bit more about him. They said that the only thing wrong with Darren was that he was a bit of a sulker, he had that side to him.

So I went away to reflect on it all and thought, 'Well look, if I go for a job that I have a great chance of getting and then suddenly I get overlooked for it, then I'm going to sulk. Sulking is only natural, it's what we humans do.' So if that was the only negative I had on Darren Ferguson, then this guy had to be taken seriously. I said to Barry, 'OK call him in for a chat.'

He came in with his brothers, and spoke about his ambitions and his desire to do well as a manager. He felt he had good qualities that could benefit the football club. One thing I have to say about Darren is that it has never been about the money, never. He was offered peanuts at the time, I think £2,000 a week, which he took without question.

After talking with Barry about Darren's interview, it was apparent that this guy was chomping at the bit to succeed, and I thought, 'Well look, he's a Ferguson, his dad is Sir Alex' and I knew that the media attention would be crazy, and we needed some positive publicity around Peterborough United.

I know Sir Alex really wanted Darren to get the job – he was constantly on the phone with Barry.

So Darren and I had a long conversation over the phone. He said what he expected, and I said what we expected, and the two kind of matched pretty well. It was obvious the guy just wanted a chance, and in my mind having a Ferguson at the helm of my football club was a massive bonus.

I got Barry to offer him the contract, and Barry came back to me to say Darren would like the evening to think about it. I said, 'Look, he either wants the job or he doesn't, I'm not messing around, you tell him I want a yes or a no.'

I think he called his dad, who told him to stop being a fucking idiot and take the job. He took the job, signed a four-year deal, and he was locked in. I had signed my first manager.

We got Darren in as a player-manager, but I don't think he ever had any intentions of playing, much to Barry's disappointment and mine. Darren was a great midfielder and would have added great experience in our soon-to-be-young side, but in fairness to Darren he wanted to concentrate on management and that's exactly what he did. He brought with him his Number 2, Kevin Russell, who had also played for Posh once upon a time, and goalkeeping coach Andy Dibble, who was obviously a well-known keeper in the football would. With this blend I felt more than confident we would make this little football club a big success.

The majority of fans at the time, I felt, thought we had got the appointment wrong. People were expecting an experienced manager and what they got was a guy who was up until that point still playing football for Wrexham and had no managerial experience at all. But I knew within time the fans would warm to Darren, and they would see that my policy from top to bottom was the way forward.

We knew it was going to be a while until we had it right on the pitch and until we got the team playing the way Darren wanted to them to play, and Darren's first match in charge was away at Lincoln City where we lost 1-0. But even from that one game it was obvious things were a bit tighter off the back of the 3-0 defeat Tommy Taylor had suffered against Stockport.

Swindon Town were next up and this was Darren's first home match at London Road. To be fair the fans gave the gaffer a great reception and this was followed by a much needed 1-1 draw. This was the first point we had picked up in eight games: we were eleventh, and seven points off of a play-off position.

We went to Bristol Rovers, and I remember us being 2-0 down and then bringing it back to 2-2: Bristol went on to knick it in the end from a free kick deep into stoppage time.

I came back to England for the Wrexham match on 10th February. This was my first time meeting the manager, and straight away we hit it off. He was my kind of guy.

Mackail-Smith was on the bench and tasted his first ten minutes of action as a Posh player coming on in the 80th minute. Boyd, McLean and an own goal gave us the 3-0 victory. It was a great performance and one that I know the gaffer would have been very pleased about given our opposition that day.

I drove over three hundred miles to see us get beaten 2-1 at Macclesfield, and remember getting abused by some of their fans. Mackail-Smith got his debut in that game. Then there was a 1-1 draw at home to Boston United with George Boyd coming on as a sub and scoring a sensational 30-yard half-volley equaliser, and his first for the club. I remember turning to my wife and saying, 'Now that's why I spent £250,000 on the white Pele!'

I wasn't happy with the performance against Boston and felt that only getting a point against them was a travesty, no disrespect to Boston. I remember coming out in the press after that game and saying I thought the players were gutless. Maybe it was the wrong thing to do, but it must have had some sort of impact because Mackail- Smith scored his first goal for the club in a 3-0 drumming away at Bury.

March couldn't have come any quicker for us with our new mentality. Two home games on the trot, a 2-0 win over Nott's County and a 4-0 win over local rivals MK Dons had put us up to ninth and only 5 points off of a play-off spot.

I felt then that this team was coming together nicely: new signings Josh Low, Craig Morgan (a young Welsh international centre-half the gaffer had played with at Wrexham – we pinched the lad from MK Dons on a free), Micah Hyde, Shane Blackett, George Boyd, Craig Mackail-Smith, Aaron McLean and Gavin Strachan (an experienced midfielder the gaffer knew well, also the son of manager Gordon Strachan) were all bedding into the side nicely. This was the new breed coming through in force!

We lost 2-1 away at Shrewsbury after going 1-0 up. We controlled that game from start to finish but allowed two soft late goals to kill us, but the trip to Grimsby Town saw us bounce back 2-0. The month finished with a 3-3 draw at Wycombe Wanderers which at that point saw us sitting in tenth position, 4 points off the playoffs, with six games left to play.

We had suddenly turned into a team who could score goals, lots of goals, and we used that to our advantage.

April saw a mixed bag of results: a disappointing 3-2 defeat away at Accrington Stanley was followed by a home game against Macclesfield Town. I remember ahead of the game I asked Darren to come up and see me. I said, 'What the fuck happened against Accrington?' and the manager lost it big time and said, 'I don't appreciate being brought up here, having to explain myself an hour before kick off of a game.' And he was right, I shouldn't have done it. At the end of the day I, like him, was new to all of this, and I had no right to take a pop at him an hour before playing our next match. But I said to Barry after Darren left the office that I had now seen the eye of the monster, as it were. I knew that when we gained success Darren would want more power, and that's not me having a dig at him, it's just his character. I knew from that point onwards that yes we would have a good relationship, but it would be tetchy at times.

We went on to beat Macclesfield 2-0 by the way, and Accrington turned out to be the last game we lost that season. We drew 1-1 with Torquay United, beat Hereford 3-0 and finished the month drawing 1-1 with Chester.

The defeat to Accrington though, in all fairness, killed us and put the chances of promotion to bed. Our final game of the season in the start of April finished 3-3. We ended that campaign tenth with 65 points on the table, 6 points from a play-off spot.

I was absolutely gutted with not gaining promotion that year, but I was so excited about the future of Peterborough United. I have no doubt in my mind whatsoever that had we started that season with the manager and team that we ended it with, it would have been a completely different story.

I knew the summer coming up was going to be the most important summer of my ownership and it was going to be a summer of changes!

THE SUMMER OF CHANGES

The first bit of business we did that summer was bring in Dean Keates and Chris Westwood from Walsall, a team that had literally just won promotion into League One. Barry knew an agent called Az, who had these two players. Westwood was a centre-half and Keates was a dynamic midfield man. When we were drawing up a list of possible targets back in April, Barry took these two names to the gaffer who replied with, 'Yeah, all day long.'

Both players were out of contract that summer, and they were both after three-year deals. Because of their ages, I think one was thirty and one was twenty-eight, I was a bit apprehensive about agreeing such a lengthy contract, but then two experienced guys like that would really add to the balance of the team.

So the decision was made and the deals were done and they were the two key signings of that summer.

Another big part of the puzzle was a kid called Charlie Lee. Charlie had been involved in the youth set up at Tottenham Hotspur and had got himself quite a reputation. His contract was coming to an end with Spurs and he had eleven different clubs chasing him. He was only twenty years old and could play at centre-half or in the middle of midfield and he was one of the first names on the gaffer's target list.

Barry met with Charlie, who, in fairness to the lad, was only interested in the football. We got the deal done and the squad was coming together nicely.

All three players were massive acquisitions for this football club, and all three deals were completed in May, because I felt it was important that all new signings needed to be in place ready for pre-season so that the guys could bond and get to know each other. We were still looking to strengthen the right-back position and a French lad called Claude Gnakpa came to light, who was at that time a free agent. Darren gave the lad a two-week trial and liked what he saw and signed him up.

We paid £50,000 for Kieran Charnock, who was a highly rated centre-half from Northwich Victoria from non-League, and then there was striker Rene Howe from Kettering Town, who was going to be back-up to the Mac attack.

We missed out on a few good players that season. Dave Edwards, who went from Shrewsbury to Wolves; Nick Bailey from Barnet, who went on to Middlesbrough via Southend for around £2 million; Simon King, who went to Gillingham; and there were a few more here and there. These were all missed due to wags or agents, but the majority of people on the gaffer's wish list that year we purchased and recruited. There were one or two players, though, on that list that I was defiantly not keen on purchasing, The manager wanted a defender called John McGreal. I said, 'You cant be serious?' This guy was around thirty-four and hadn't played football for the last two years. 'Bring him out to Spain and we'll see what he's like.' To which the gaffer said, 'We've tried, but he won't come until he signs the deal.' John McGreal never played football again.

Another one was Ritchie Barker, who was a striker at Hartlepool. I looked up his stats and saw that he was a 1 in 5 goal scorer, which for me wasn't good enough. I think again Richard Barker went on to drop out of the League and didn't score again after that conversation. That's juts two examples of our disagreements over players, but those kinds of conversations were healthy for our relationship to work and it worked both ways.

One player that I brought to Darren's attention was Chris Whelpdale. I received a phone call from one of my friends who goes and watches a fair few non-League games. He called me from Billericay and said,

'Darragh, you've gotta buy Billericay's outside right, he's unbelievable. He's young, quick, good with the football and would be an awesome signing for Peterborough United.'

So I called Barry and the Gaffer and said, 'Chris Whelpdale, Billericay, he's £15,000, sign him up!' Chris turned out to be a great signing for the club and was an important cog in the wheel.

I paid £40,000 that year to bring the squad over to Spain to a luxury 5-star resort called La Cala. This was to be a place where the team could train all week in perfect conditions, get familiar with each other and gel.

Once a year in Spain my company would have a huge summer party on Silk's Beach, and I would pay for about five hundred of my employees to come out and celebrate. This one just happened to fall in place with the final day of the training camp, so I invited all the team down for that to let their hair down at the end of what had been a very busy week. I think everyone returned to their hotel rooms at bout 8 o'clock the next morning, so I'm sure everyone had a great time. The only hitch was when a member of our staff, without naming anybody, fell on top of the coach driver in the early hours whilst trying to drive the coach back to the hotel.

That summer our aim was to win League Two. Barry was to be a busy boy getting rid of the players we didn't see a future for: Futcher, Butcher, Gain, Benjamin, Crow, etc. were all on, or soon to be on, their way. We had completely turned the club upside down. The new manager was brought in and it was like he had a clean paintbrush, it was the perfect job for him as his first, and it was exciting times for all of us involved.

LEAGUE TWO: GET ME OUT OF HERE

Expectations were high, very high, and I had spent a lot of money to get us to a point where I felt confident we could finally achieve some success. We had an exciting young Ferguson at the reigns and an equally exciting young team capable of anything.

We started the season away at Rochdale where we won 3-0, and this was followed by a live Sky game against Southampton in the League cup, who we beat 2-1. We received £100,000 for that game thanks to Sky.

It couldn't have been a better start.

And then suddenly our first away game to Rotherham we got smashed 3-1. I remember us going 3-0 down and then Aaron getting a late goal. It was horrible, and a bit of a reality check.

Next up we faced Chesterfield at London Road, which again we lost 3-2 and it was becoming apparent even at that stage in the season that we needed a new keeper, someone who could dominate the box.

This had been a process going through our minds for a little while now, but because Mark Tyler had done such a great service for the club, and given the fact that the fans adored him, we felt we should give him a fair crack. But with the way we had been the defeated over the last couple of games this thought had now come to the forefront of my mind, and it wasn't going away.

Next we had West Brom at home in the League Cup which we lost 2-0. We found a win at Accrington 2-0, Nottingham Forest in the Johnston's Paint Trophy we won 3-2, and we beat Mansfield Town 2-1.

Then we went to Bradford and lost 1-0. At this point we were ninth and 4 points off the top spot.

Next up was Morecambe. This was to be a frustrating day and turned out to be a bit of a game changer for us.

Morecambe had just come up that year from non-League, and we drew 1-1, but Man of the Match that day was the Morecambe shot-stopper, a player on loan from Norwich. I believe his name was Joe Lewis. I remember this result proper pissed me off, so much so that I went downstairs into the manager's office and said 'Guys, what the fuck is going on?'

At which the manager got stuck in, Rooster got stuck in, and everyone was throwing opinions across the room.

Rooster was saying, 'They're not experienced enough, they're too young, they're making the same fucking mistakes, and the strikers ain't doing this and the strikers ain't doing that...'

At that time there was a big debate going on in whether Aaron and Craig could actually play together, given the fact that they were so similar. I was in the camp that said they could, the manager was in the camp that said they couldn't, although I think maybe that was more his coach's influence than his. I said, 'Look, if you give these guys a good run they will adapt and learn to play together and both become prolific strikers for this football club as a duo.' I knew this would be the case. I said, 'Anyway, it's not just about the fucking strikers, it's not just about the team being young. We have experience in there too, we've got Micah Hyde, Dean Keates, Chris Westwood, Josh Low, there is experience in the team.'

It was an argument that erupted from nothing, and eventually it died down and we agreed that we needed to start winning games again, get back on track and become more consistent.

Before fans start panicking about a little ruckus like this: relax, they happen at every football club in the country. It's a result of having a bunch of ambitious and passionate people who work for your club.

We played Darlington next and I remember entering the ground and I was in awe, their boardroom, their stadium was stunning, it was like walking into a Premier League club. I remember we went out there and played really well and sneaked a point by scoring in the last minute. It was such a great point to get because for 80-odd minutes we were dead and buried.

Next up was Shrewsbury, who were also in their brand new stadium, and it actually fell on the same day I had that fisticuffs meeting with CH. I had to drive all the way from London to Shrewsbury to make kick off. We won the match 2- 0 thanks to a worldy goal from Charlie Lee who was now on four for the season, and then finished off by George Boyd.

We beat Grimsby 2-1, lost 3-1 against MK Dons in the John Player Trophy, beat Wycombe 2-1, then drew 1-1 with Lincoln and 1-1 with Hereford.

November was to be a great month, we actually won four of our five games, losing to Bury away in between.

We carried on the momentum going into December, winning the first three games. We beat Staines Town in the FA cup 5-0, Nott's County 1-0 and Chester 2-1. We then had a top of the table clash with MK Dons, they were top with 41 points and we were second with 37 points. To my frustration we lost 2-1.

We then had Mansfield Town and Morecambe away. I drove to both matches in my Bentley and really clocked up the miles. At Mansfield I remember going into the boardroom and their chairman came up to me and said, 'We're fucked, both of our centre-halves are injured.' Barry and I looked at each other. I hated it when people said shit like that ahead of a match, because it always had a habit of biting us on the arse, and this was to prove my point. We lost 2-0. No disrespect to Mansfield, but we needed to be battering teams like that if we wanted to win the League. At this point MK Dons were flying away at the top.

We went to Morecambe, and raced into an early 2-0 lead. We did something I never expected us to do and scored twice in quick succession from corners, both headers. I went outside at half-time for a smoke, and a Morecambe fan said to me, 'Whoever scores the next goal will win.' I remember thinking to myself, Are you off your fucking head? We were cruising at 2-0. Morecambe scored the next goal and went on to win 3-2.

From the whole game the only thing I remember is their goalkeeper making two of the best fucking saves I've ever seen in my life, two double saves off the line from Craig, and it was Joe Lewis again.

I always remember the manager had a list of the best young up-and-coming goalkeepers in the country, and Joe's name was on that list. After the match I saw the gaffer and I said, 'Look, what do you want to do about Joe Lewis?' The manager said, 'We'll never get him, no chance!' I called Barry and I said 'Joe Lewis?' 'No chance,' Barry said. 'Norwich won't sell him!' I said, 'Barry, we need a top young goalkeeper, no disrespect to Tyler, but we need a top shot-stopper with age on his side.' 'Chairman, Norwich will not sell the lad and plus Joe Lewis will not come to Peterborough United.' I said 'Barry, get in your car, and drive to fucking Norwich and find out what Glen Roeder wants to do with this young goalkeeper.'

I remember being at my house in Sunningdale when Barry called and said 'Listen, you've got no fucking chance. Glen Roeder is saying the only way they will sell him is for £400,000 and not a penny less!'

This kid was only fucking nineteen, he had played a few games at League level with Morecambe, his value was fuck-all really, zero, but he had played at England Under 17 and Under 18 level, he was 6ft 6, everyone in the game said this young lad was going to go places. He was everything we were looking for in a keeper: big, great presence, and on top of that his reflex saves were phenomenal.

I said, 'Right, tell them we'll split the payments over forty months and we'll buy him today!' Barry said, 'Really?' I said, 'Yes fucking really, do the deal and don't come back from Norwich without the deal being done!'

Barry called the next day to say the deal had been done, and he was meeting Joe and his dad later that afternoon to get things completed. This had made my day!

The team went into January wanting to get back to winning ways and it came with back-to-back wins over Shrewsbury and Colchester. Joe and his dad actually came to the Colchester match and he signed his contract ahead of the Macclesfield game which was to be his debut. This was another massive part of the puzzle complete. We had just signed an England Under 21 goalkeeper, who in four, maybe five years time could be worth £3 million to us.

I appreciate many Posh fans didn't take to Joe, and he never did go on to be sold for mega money. However, we had multiple chances to cash in on him and the timing was never right for one reason or another. Probably one of most disappointing things in my time as owner was to not see Joe realise his potential with us and us to earn serious money from it or cash out at the right time.

We were sixth at this point in the League and 14 points behind MK Dons, we were dragging our arses. We had won thirteen and lost eight and were far too inconsistent for my liking. We lost to Macclesfield that day who were bottom of League Two. The fans weren't happy and we were 14 points off the summit.

I called the manager and said, 'Look do you wanna get out of League Two? Do you wanna win this League or not?' He said, 'What do you mean?' I said, 'Do you wanna win this fucking League?' He said, 'Yes, of course I do!' I said, 'Right, then, it's time for siege mentality. It's not about the first half of the season, its about the second half. Your dad always talks about siege mentality, so why don't you go and find some fucking siege mentality! We're meant to be the big spenders in this League, everyone's giving us flack, we're in sixth place, I ain't happy, you ain't happy, we need to be insular here and shut out the rest of the world. We need to be going out there and smacking the shit out of all these football teams and beating them badly, none of this fucking 1-0 here, 2-1 there and then lose the occasional one!'

I said, 'Can you fucking do that?' 'Course I can!' he replied. 'Your dad's a great second-half-of-the-season manager, why don't you go out there and prove you're a chip off the old fucking block! I'm going back to the States, I'll call you in a few days,' I concluded.

The next game was against Accrington Stanley. I think we demolished them! 8 fucking 2. It was the day the holy trinity came to the forefront, they scored the lot, Boydy got a hat trick, Aaron got a hat trick and Craig scored twice.

Of course it wouldn't be us if we didn't let the opposition have a couple – we like to give teams a sniff.

We continued adding to the squad in January: Tom Williams, who was an experienced left-back from Wycombe Wanderers, who we got on a free, and Liam Hatch, who we paid £150,000 for from Barnet.

I didn't really want to do the Hatch deal but the gaffer was persistent. He felt we needed a target man, someone different to Aaron and Craig. I've never been a fan of target men, but I backed my manager.

In fairness to Hatchey, he scored a great goal against his former club Barnet, and their chairman 'Tony' who is a top guy lost his rag big time. Apparently Barry had verbally agreed with them that we wouldn't play Liam Hatch in that game, unbeknown to the manager and myself, and of course Hatchey came off the bench and scored a great long-range goal from 25 yards. We won the game 1-0.

We lost to West Brom 3-0 in the FA cup, and then we just put our foot down big time and went on a fifteen game unbeaten run through April and March. The wins were:

Rotherham	3-1
Wrexham	0-0
Chesterfield	2-1
Barnet	1-0
Macclesfield	3-0
Wrexham	2-0
Bury	1-0
Barnet	2-0
Dagenham	3-2
Brentford	2-1
Nott's County	0-0
MK Dons	1-1
Chester	1-0
Lincoln City	4-0
Wycombe	2-2

We were flying high and at this point we were sitting at the top of the tree, 1 point clear of MK Dons on 86 points. Remember before this run the Dons had been 14 points clear of us, so we had actually caught them up!

Ahead of the Stockport game I said to the manager, 'Keep your eyes out for Stockport's left winger Tommy Rowe.' I really rated him. I knew their manager Jim Gannon was banging on about how good this kid was. He had scored a lot of their goals that season and the ones he hadn't scored he had created. 'Who?' the gaffer replied. Stockport beat us 1-0 that day, to end our fifteen-game unbeaten run, and who scored the goal? Tommy fucking Rowe. I remember after the final whistle the manager looked up to me in the stands as if to say, 'Why did you mention his name!' But from then on we knew we wanted to sign Tommy.

We beat Hereford at their place, winning 1-0 with a looping header from the 5ft Dean Keates. This goal gained us promotion into League One. After the match the team celebrated on pitch with the fans, it was fantastic. I was over in the States at that point so I was absolutely gutted not to be there, but the manager pulled himself away from the celebrations to give me a call, and we chatted for five minutes and had a little moment, which was nice. Although we had not won the League, we had achieved the target in getting out of it, which was far more important.

We beat Grimsby away 4-1 and then ended on a sour note losing to Darlington 2-0 at home. I remember the gaffer had the boys in the dressing room after that game and ripped them all a new arsehole. We finished the season in second place with 92 points, 5 points from MK Dons.

People said to me after the Hereford win, at the end of those 90 minutes, what was going through your head? Do you know what my answer was? Next.

HOW THE TABLE LOOKED

Pos	Name	P	W	D	L	F	A	W	D	L	F	A	GD	PTS
1	MK Dons	46	11	7	5	39	17	18	3	2	43	20	+45	97
2	Peterborough	46	14	4	5	46	20	14	4	5	38	23	+41	92
3	Hereford	46	11	6	6	34	19	15	4	4	38	22	+31	88
4	Stockport	46	11	5	7	40	30	13	5	5	32	24	+18	82
5	Rochdale	46	11	4	8	37	28	12	7	4	40	26	+23	80
6	Darlington	46	11	7	5	36	22	11	5	7	31	18	+27	78
7	Wycombe	46	13	6	4	29	15	9	6	8	27	27	+14	78
8	Chesterfield	46	9	8	6	42	29	10	4	9	34	27	+20	69
9	Rotherham	46	12	4	7	37	29	9	7	7	25	29	+4	64
10	Bradford City	46	10	4	9	30	30	7	7	9	33	31	+2	62
11	Morecambe	46	9	6	8	33	32	7	6	10	26	31	-4	60
12	Barnet	46	10	6	7	37	30	6	6	11	19	33	-7	60
13	Bury	46	8	6	9	30	30	8	5	10	28	31	-3	59
14	Brentford	46	7	5	11	25	35	10	3	10	27	35	-18	59
15	Lincoln City	46	9	3	11	33	38	9	1	13	28	39	-16	58
16	Grimsby Town	46	7	5	11	26	34	8	5	10	29	32	-11	55
17	Accrington	46	7	1	15	20	39	9	2	12	29	44	-34	51
18	Shrewsbury	46	9	6	8	31	22	3	8	12	25	43	-9	50
19	Macclesfield	46	6	8	9	27	31	5	9	9	20	33	-17	50
20	Dagenham & R	46	6	7	10	27	32	7	3	13	22	38	-21	49
21	Notts County	46	8	5	10	19	23	2	13	8	18	30	-16	48
22	Chester FC	46	5	5	13	21	30	7	6	10	30	38	-17	47
23	Mansfield Town	46	6	3	14	30	39	5	6	12	18	29	-20	42
24	Wrexham	46	6	7	10	16	28	4	3	16	22	42	-32	40

AGAINST ALL ODDS

A week or two after the season had finished, I took Darren, Rooster, Barry and the clubs CEO Bob Symns out to the Bahamas for a week to discuss the following seasons targets. It was also a great way of me rewarding them for their efforts through the long League Two campaign.

I knew from the off that we would get out of League One. With the money I had invested and with the way the manager had got the team playing, I just knew that it would happen. For my money it was going to be back-to-back promotions all day long.

I walked out to the pool one afternoon, and Barry was tanning himself on a sun bed as he does, frightening everyone in the vicinity in his thong. Darren and Rooster were sitting round the corner looking through loads of paperwork. I asked them what they were doing and they explained that they were looking through all the teams in League, seeing which we could beat and which we might struggle against. The manager said, 'I think we have a really good chance of the play-offs this year.' I said, 'What do you mean? Playoffs? Are you fucking kidding me? We can win League One!' At which they both looked at me like I had two heads. 'No chance,' they said. 'Not in this League.' I said, 'Look, I'm not being funny, but I expect us to get promotion and if anything challenge for the title. That's my mandate for you guys this season!' I think they had looked at the League and saw the likes of Leeds United, Leicester City, Millwall, Scunthorpe, etc., and thought, No chance. I was the only person that summer that felt we could achieve the impossible, back to back.

We strengthened the squad as always. The manager had Paul Coutts as one of his main targets and I remember worrying about this because he was playing in the Scottish Highland Leagues at the time. I think Cove Rangers wanted £25,000 for the boy, and I remember the manager saying to me, 'Look, if you're not sure about him, I'll pay his transfer fee and you can give me it back if he turns out to be a success.'

I was never going to let the manager pay his own money to buy players, and the gaffer uses that card on me from time to time. He knows I'm not going to let him pay, it's his way of getting round me.

We secured Scott Rendell for over £100,000, after joining us on loan the previous season. He was a prolific striker from Cambridge United, and again this was for back-up on the Mac attack. Liam Hatch and Rene Howe hadn't gone to plan so we needed to keep our options open.

I remember that summer Darren's Number 1 target was an Argentinean from Wycombe Wanderers called Sergio Torres, and it still annoys me to this day, because I didn't want Sergio to sign for Peterborough United. I knew he was a flair player, but the guy was always injured. He had only played about eighteen games the previous season due to injuries, and Wycombe wanted a lot of money for him. But I backed the manager and we signed Sergio Torres along with right-back Russell Martin for a total of £200,000. Barry actually brought Russell Martin to the table, and Barry being Barry secured the lad on £1,000 a week, which was a great deal for the football club. We paid Wycombe £50,000 for him.

Sergio on his own cost the club £150,000 and arrived needing an operation to his foot, believe it or not.

Dominic Green was a talent that we had spotted at Dagenham. He was actually in Huddersfield, and about to sign for them when we called him and got him to come over.

We pushed strong for Dominic, and even to this day players will tell you the lad was one of the most skilful players in training, but for whatever reason the penny didn't drop, and that's what happens in football.

We paid £150,000 for Dominic Green. I remember his debut, he came off the bench and turned the game on its arse, scored a goal and hit the post from a free kick, but unfortunately we weren't to see many of those performances from him. If you ask me for disappointments during my reign, Dominic would be one of my biggest.

Shaun Batt was on Darren's radar, a striker/winger from non-League Fisher Athletic. Barry did the deal, and he cost us £5,000 and was on £400 a week. Job done. It was another non-league punt, and if you think about it we ended up making £350,000 on him when we sold him on to Millwall in January 2010.

People may laugh at our trials and errors with strikers over the years but remember that on the back of the previous season Aaron and Craig were hot property. Aaron had won the golden boot and was the highest-scoring player in Great Britain, Craig had scored nineteen goals. Between them they had about fifty-five goals in all competitions, and were the hottest strike partnership outside the Premier League.

Now that summer, as we were pushing for the drive into League One, Wolves came sniffing around, literally. I met with Aaron before going out to the Bahamas and he made it very clear to me he wanted to leave Peterborough United and be allowed to speak with Wolves. I made it very clear to Aaron that I wanted more money than Wolves were offering. In hindsight maybe I should have let him go, because the money Wolves were offering was more than he went for to Hull, but it scared the shit out of me because I didn't want to be breaking the team up.

The manager actually told me to sell Aaron, but to me this wasn't the right time and the Mac attack needed to stay together in order for us to get promoted from League One.

In the weeks after that I had a few falling-outs with Aaron's agent, and I knew Aaron was moping around a bit. I came out in the press and said that Aaron wanted to leave, etc., etc., and I don't think Aaron liked that. I don't think he wanted it to go public because he was so popular with the fans, but me being me I like being honest, I felt it right they know.

I said to Aaron, 'I know you want what's right for you, but I want what's right for this football club, and you're a massive part of my plans in getting out of League One. Wolves are in the Championship (as they were at the time) and you'll get the chance to play at that level with us.' In the end we kissed and made up, he signed a new four-year deal and we made him the highest-paid player at the club.

We ended Josh Low's contract, which was the manager's decision. Josh still had about four years left of his contract and I did something I had never done before. Josh is still on our wage bill to this day! If we had paid him off at the time it would have cost us hundreds and hundreds of thousands, so we did a deal to stop the rot. He was an expensive mistake, which happens in football, and one that could have cost us a lot more.

Claude Gnakpa's contract was coming up and his agent was a prick. We offered Claude more money but he wanted silly money. I think our decision was justified in the end because he ended up dropping out of the League and going to non-League Luton Town.

Mark Tyler we shipped out on loan to Hull City, which was a great move for him. We released Danny Crow, I was never a big lover of the lad and he had a massive attitude, he always felt he should be higher than he actually was. We had a top League Two club offer us big money for Danny, but his agent turned his nose up at it. We ended up paying his contract up and again he went on to drop out of the League. Frustrating thing with young lads like Crowey is that he had so much talent, but like many others have shown, talent doesn't always get you to the top!

Apart from that the summer was pretty quiet. We had done good business and felt ready for the next step.

I remember we started the season pretty badly, losing 1-0 to Southend and then 2-1 to Bristol City in the League Cup. We then had a great performance against Leyton Orient beating them 3-0 with the Mac attack grabbing all three goals.

That win was then followed by two further defeats, 1-0 to Scunthorpe and 2-1 to Hartlepool. After these four games we were sitting in twentieth position, 7 points off the summit.

I was beside myself. Bristol City had ended our cup run and the league table looked horrendous! Shane Blackett, who had started off as a good player for us, was always injured and couldn't find form and

Chris Westwood's legs had gone according to our coaches. Defensively we looked shot.

We played Bristol Rovers and beat them 5-4. It showed how dangerous we were going forward, but again highlighted how poor we were defensively.

The manager came to me after the match, and said he was interested in signing a centre-half from Fulham by the name of Gabriel Zakuani. We did a deal with Fulham where we took over his wages in order to take him on loan until January. Gabby was on big, big money and had been sold as a teenager for £1 million from Leyton Orient. The manager spoke with Tony Pulis, who had Gabby on loan at Stoke and had played him at right-back for nineteen games or something, and Tony spoke very highly of Gabby, so we did the deal. Looking back now, this was probably one of the gaffer's shrewdest moves in the loan market as Gabby has been magnificent for our club and is still only twenty-five years old.

Gabby debuted at Northampton in the 1-1 draw. We then drew again 2-2 with Tranmere. The next two games coming up were against MK Dons and Leeds, two big games. I still wasn't happy with our performances of late and decided to try some kidology to give the gaffer and his staff a kick up the arse. I contacted Barry and gave him a sheet of paper which had four different manager's names on it. I told him to give it to the gaffer and to tell him that I wasn't happy with the way things were going at the minute and that he needed to win the next three games.

I had no intention of firing the manager, but I wanted to stick a rocket up his arse, so I told Barry to play the game. I like to do that sometimes to motivate people, sometimes it works and sometimes it doesn't.

Half an hour later I get a phone call from Barry saying, 'Fucking hell, Chairman, what have ya done?' I said, 'Why, what's happened?' He said, 'He's fucking exploded, he's out on the pitch talking to his dad.' 'Why's he talking to his dad?' I said. 'Well, he's obviously asking for his advice on the situation,' Barry replied. 'Fuck me, you're kidding, it was only meant to give him a kick up the arse!' I said. Next I had a call from the gaffer: 'Chairman, I don't understand, Barry came in and gave me a bit of paper with a list of managers on it.' I said, 'Gaffer, it's just my way of geeing you up.' 'Well you have a fucking funny way of trying to gee me up,' he said. I said, 'Darren, you've gotta get your act together, we're better than this, we have two key games coming up, games that we can win. You have to start believing we can get promotion, that's all I'm trying to do. I'm trying to light a torch here, light a flame.' I ended it with, 'Now calm down, I'm not sacking you or anything.'

I flew back to the UK for the MK Dons match and to my delight we beat them 2-1 on their turf. I actually did a Pete Winkleman after the game and went pitchside to high-five all the players, etc.

Next up was a massive game against Leeds United. Gary MacAlister completely dismissed us, it was a sell-out attendance and the boys worked their socks off. We battered them 2-0, it was a great fucking win. We lost to Dagenham 1-0 in the Johnstones Paint Trophy but then beat Walsall 2-1, and I believe those three League victories were a massive change in the sands for us. At the end of it, it gave belief to the players that we could stand on our own two feet in this League and compete with the big boys. With Gabby now the rock in our defence, we suddenly looked a force to be reckoned with.

This new belief installed into the players created a sixteen-game unbeaten run in the League, other results being:

Carlisle	3-3
Brighton	0-0
Huddersfield	4-0
Crewe	1-1
Hereford	2-0
Yeovil	1-0
Colchester	2-1
Swindon	2-2
Stockport	3-1
Oldham	2-2

At this stage we were fourth in the League and we were flying. We then came to a sudden halt at Leicester in December where we were thrashed 4-0, we got absolutely fucking hammered. I was that unhappy with the performance that I actually left ten minutes before the final whistle.

We finished December with two wins, 1-0 at home to Millwall and 6-3 away to Cheltenham.

We sold Micah Hyde back in the November, who had obviously been a big part of the previous year's success and of course he was our captain, but we didn't really have a choice. His legs had gone and he couldn't really keep up with the demands of the League. For me this was an easy decision but for the manager it was a big deal, the pair got on really well and I know that Darren found that particular decision hard. But I knew that to get Paul Coutts playing, and to bring out his potential, Micah had to be sacrificed. I said to the gaffer, 'Look, he's on nearly £4,000 a week, he's thirty-four, you need to be cruel to be kind. Let's get Barry to get a deal done to get him out.'

Darren is no different to any manager in that he will protect his players, and he didn't want to see what other people were seeing in regards to Micah's drop in form. In the end Micah was released from the club and Paul Coutts came into his own. We singed Gabby permanently for around £280,000 and with add-ons and everything else the deal was to reach £380,000, but it was money well spent and we were happy to have him.

We were still looking for a midfield man that could bring goals to the table and Lee Frecklington was the player we had in mind. Lee I think actually got misquoted in saying Peterborough would be a sideways move for himself, but that was rubbish because Lee actually wanted to come to us and we wanted Lee and when the deal happened it took the lad about six minutes to sign on the dotted line. But in January we secured him on loan.

We also brought in Andrew Crofts from Gillingham, and James Chester from Manchester United. James was the first Man Utd player that the manager had actually brought in. I remember when we first secured Darren as manager I expected to see him use his father to his favour, but in fairness to Darren he wanted to do it his own way and I've never been bitter about that.

I remember just before Christmas we were trying to sign a striker. I wanted Danny Graham from Carlisle, or Jamie Ward from Chesterfield, but the manager didn't want Jamie Ward. He contacted Gareth Southgate in regards to Danny Graham. Gareth had had Danny on loan at Middlesbrough. Gareth's words were 'Na, he won't be good enough for ya.'

Danny Graham went on to play for Watford and then Swansea in the Premier League, and Jamie Ward went on to Sheffield United and Derby County.

We also tried to buy Anthony Pilkington for £400,000 but Huddersfield pipped us to the post and paid the same money.

In hindsight we were getting carried away. With all the new signings now secured the place was costing me in excess of £250,000 a *month* to run. We were signing far too many players and not getting enough out of the door. The squad was bulging at the seams, never mind the wage bill getting bigger by the week.

We had an average January and average February with the low point being the 3-1 loss to Yeovil Town. I remember the losses around that time always had Joe Lewis at the centre of a lot of the mistakes being made, and at Yeovil in particular he had a right stinker. After the match the manager and his management team came up and I said to them, 'What's going on with Joe Lewis?'

It turned into a massive argument with the manager saying, 'Don't speak to me like I'm one of your minions.'

To which I replied 'If you speak to me like that again I'll put you through that fucking door!'

It got very, very heated indeed. In the end it died down and I suggested to Darren that he send Joe to Manchester for a week to train with United's goalkeeping coach Eric Steele. In fairness it was probably the best thing Joe did, because he spent a very important week there and came back all revitalised and found top form after that. The argument must have been positive because we had a fucking phenomenal March! We played six games that month and won the lot:

Leyton Orient	3-2
Hartlepool	2-1
Scunthorpe	2-1
Northampton	1-0
Bristol Rovers	1-0
Leicester City	2-0

After this run we found ourselves in second place with 78 points, 4 points from Leicester City who were on the top spot. Leicester had found a poor run of form and only a month earlier had been 11 points clear at the top.

We beat Oldham 2-1 away and suddenly we found ourselves only 2 points from Leicester. I honestly felt that this would be our year to gain a trophy, we were on fire. We had created a nice little run of seven wins on the trot, and Leicester were buckling under the pressure.

We then drew 1-1 with Cheltenham and lost 2-0 to Millwall. Leicester had been picking points up again and we were now 7 points adrift. A win against Stockport had us in second position with 85 points.

After the Stockport match we did a deal with their acting chairman to buy Tommy Rowe. The club were going into administration at that point and I smelt blood. Stockport wanted £750,000 and we gave them £260,000 and the deal was complete. We were sitting second in the League with 85 points, with MK Dons behind us on 81 points: they were our only threat to gaining automatic promotion.

We always felt it would go to the Swindon game, that to get promotion we would need to beat Swindon at home. We were due to play Colchester away with MK Dons playing Walsall on the same day at Stadium MK; both Colchester and Walsall we middle of the table and I expected both MK Dons and ourselves to win comfortably.

So for us to get promoted at Colchester we needed to beat them and Walsall would have to beat MK Dons at Stadium MK.

I remember it was a good performance from us and Charlie Lee scored a fantastic goal to put us 1-0 up. Midway through the match the atmosphere suddenly changed from being the usual kind of crowd atmosphere to all-out excitement from the Posh end. I said to Barry, 'What the fuck's going on?' We honestly didn't even consider promotion at that game. Barry rang his son and was told that Walsall had gone 1-0 up at Stadium MK.

When the final whistle blew at Colchester, I remember saying to Barry, 'What was the final score at MK?' and it turned out the game was still going on.

I went down to the touchline to wait for news, when a BBC journalist said to me, 'It's over, you've been promoted.' So I told the manager, and he goes charging onto the pitch, the whole team are celebrating and going mad, but unbeknownst to me there had been a terrible injury at Stadium MK and the teams were still playing with 6 minutes of added on time. It was all on Sky Sports Soccer Saturday, that MK Dons and Walsall still playing and we were all fucking celebrating. If MK had got an equaliser, we would have looked like the biggest idiots on earth... But hey, it was a momentous occasion.

I called Natalie to say what had just happened. She was due to fly in for the Swindon game for the celebrations, as we didn't expect the party to start early. But myself, the players and management all celebrated on the pitch in front of fans, who turned out in force, by the way.

We then went to London Road to end the season against Swindon. I actually watched the first half from the London Road Terrace with the fans. We had a really big day of celebrations. We drew the game 2-2 and after the 90 minutes we handed all the medals out on the pitch. It was another fantastic day that won't be forgotten in a hurry.

I was then left thinking, Wow, back-to-back promotions! As always, my first thoughts were, Right, what's next? Remember I took over Peterborough United against all the odds, with everyone telling me I shouldn't do it and that I'm a dreamer, and now suddenly we are a Championship football club. We had achieved something that had never been achieved in the club's long history, back-to-back promotions!

HOW THE TABLE LOOKED

Pos	Name	P	W	D	L	F	A	W	D	L	F	A	GD	PTS
1	Leicester City	46	13	9	1	41	16	14	6	3	43	23	+45	96
2	Peterborough	46	14	6	3	41	22	12	5	6	37	32	+24	89
3	MK Dons	46	12	4	7	42	25	14	5	4	41	22	+36	87
4	Leeds United	46	17	2	4	49	20	9	4	10	28	29	+28	84
5	Millwall	46	13	4	6	30	21	12	3	8	33	32	+10	82
6	Scunthorpe	46	13	5	5	44	24	9	5	9	38	39	+19	76
7	Tranmere	46	15	5	3	41	20	6	6	11	21	29	+13	74
8	Southend	46	13	2	8	29	20	8	6	9	29	41	-3	71
9	Huddersfield	46	9	8	6	32	28	9	6	8	30	37	-3	68
10	Oldham	46	9	9	5	35	24	7	8	8	31	41	+1	65
11	Bristol Rovers	46	11	4	8	44	29	6	8	9	35	32	+18	63
12	Colchester	46	7	4	12	21	24	11	5	7	37	34	0	63
13	Walsall	46	10	3	10	34	36	7	7	9	27	30	-5	61
14	Leyton Orient	46	6	6	11	24	33	9	5	9	21	24	-12	56
15	Swindon Town	46	8	7	8	37	34	4	10	9	31	37	-3	53
16	Brighton	46	6	6	11	32	40	7	7	9	23	30	-15	52
17	Yeovil Town	46	6	10	7	26	29	6	5	12	15	37	-25	51
18	Stockport	46	9	7	7	34	28	7	5	11	25	29	+2	50
19	Hartlepool	46	8	7	8	45	40	5	4	14	21	39	-13	50
20	Carlisle	46	8	7	8	36	32	4	7	12	20	37	-13	50
21	Northampton	46	8	8	7	38	29	4	5	14	23	36	-4	49
22	Crewe	46	8	4	11	30	38	4	6	13	29	44	-23	46
23	Cheltenham	46	7	6	10	30	38	2	6	15	21	53	-40	39
24	Hereford	46	6	4	13	23	28	3	3	17	19	51	-37	34

NOW A CHAMPIONSHIP CLUB CHAIRMAN

After the League One promotion I was looking forward to enjoying the summer and excited about planning for the Championship season ahead. Unfortunately it started off on the wrong footing. QPR approached Darren Ferguson with regard to his availability, and he rang me and he said, 'Look, I've been approached by QPR and I'd like to think about the job.' And that pissed me off. I said, 'Right, OK, that's not the response I expected.' He went on to say, 'Well I kind of want to think about the offer, can you please not tell anyone about it?' The first thing I did was ring Barry because I wanted to find out where we stood legally. I said 'He's asked me not to mention it to anyone.' Barry said, 'Well, they have to contact the club before approaching Darren legally, there is a process. I will contact QPR.'

So Barry rang QPR, who said they were interested but they weren't making an offer, so I think they had gone through the back door via Darren's agent.

A day or so later Darren came back to me and said he didn't want to go to QPR, but by that point I was angered just by the fact that Darren had wanted to talk to them. In hindsight maybe I should have allowed him to speak with them; it's only right that a young manager gets the time to think about progressing their career at a bigger club. I should have handled it differently but I didn't. At the time I acted possessively.

I think I likened it to my wife wanting time to try out a new man, and then a few days later coming back to me saying, 'Nah, I'm not interested in him, I think I'll stay with you.' West Brom sniffed around, and then

Reading made a phone call to the club enquiring about Darren Ferguson. Nicky Hammond spoke with Barry who of course said no way, and in any case Reading didn't want to pay any compensation. Darren was miffed about why he wasn't given the opportunity to speak with Reading.

So it was now always in the back of my mind as to whether he actually wanted to be here or not. I didn't like his name being linked to these jobs and I didn't like seeing his name in the paper every fucking day a new job came up.

I remember we went off to La Cala again in July. It was a time when a lot of things were going on in my life personally. Off the field, some of my businesses were struggling. It was probably a good job that we were in the Championship that season because I felt I wouldn't need to put so much money into the club personally.

All I wanted was a pretty low-key season in all fairness, but me being me I started banging on about wanting three promotions, and therein lies what probably set the tone for that very bad season. Expectations were high, my expectations were high, I was living in fantasyland and I had underestimated how difficult the Championship would be, but then I wasn't alone on this.

Back in June, but after the Reading fiasco, the gaffer came to my office in Spain and we spent a few hours together. I'm not saying our relationship was frayed, but it certainly wasn't anywhere near as good as it was previously.

It became clear that Darren wanted a new contract, and wherever I seemed to go around the club at that point it was, 'Oh, we're in the Championship now, chairman!'

Players' agents were all going crazy on the phone: 'Our player deserves a new contract, he's a Championship player now.' The management staff all wanted new contracts: 'We're in the Championship, we're in the Championship.'

I remember saying to everyone, 'Yes, we are in the Championship, but we haven't begun playing in the Championship yet. So we have earnt our spot, but let's go out there and show that we deserve to be there, let's not get ahead of ourselves.'

I got ahead of myself, I know the manager got ahead of himself. We thought that because of our desire to go forward and our ability to score goals, we didn't need to worry about the defence and the fact we were shipping in goals, we would outscore any opposition.

Whilst in La Cala, I gave the manager and all of his staff new improved 4 year contracts to reflect the fact that we were in the Championship, but something in my gut was telling me not to give them at that point. I wanted to wait and see how we bedded into the League, get a few games under our belts, work hard and then look at contract extensions at Christmas.

These contracts were hefty increases, players wanted hefty increases and signing players was just the same, everybody wanted big money.

When you're a League One, League Two club it's easy to negotiate contracts, but as soon as you're in the Championship people see it as big money. But what they don't realise is that Peterborough United being in the Championship is different to, say, Bradford being in the Championship, where they go from average crowds of 10,000 in League One to 20,000 in the Championship. We had average crowds of around 5,000 in League One and that was likely to increase by 2,000 if we were lucky, so financially from that point of view it didn't make a lot of difference. Where it does make a difference is with the TV monies received, but if you give all your TV money away in management and player contracts, etc., it leaves very little else to do business with.

So with my gut feeling telling me not to give these new contracts, I did so on the basis of our back-to-back promotions. They needed rewarding, plus there was the fact that I had stopped Darren from talking to Reading, so I wanted to stop all this speculation. I thought that by giving Darren a new four-year deal it would put all these rumours to bed.

He was linked with Reading, QPR, Wigan, West Brom, and I don't like living with uncertainty, I wanted it to come to a stop. Something told me from that point onwards that everything was going to go downhill, and this was on top of everything going wrong for me business-wise.

We signed Toumani Diagouraga, a name the manager wanted as his Number 1 target. We spent nearly £300,000 bringing that lad in from

Hereford, and it didn't feel right from my point of view. We had been chasing him for a long time and being that Dave (as we called him) and his agent were French, there were a lot of communication break-downs. When he did sign, he showed glimpses, but the lad had come to the club with a lot of personal baggage and I don't think that helped him at all.

Frecklington signed for us permanently and actually turned out to be one of our better players at championship level: we turned down big money for him that year from Swansea.

We ended the buying with Danny Mills and Romone McCrae, two seventeen-year-olds from Crawley Town. They were both punts in an attempt to get the youth set-up going. The thoughts were to get them in playing regularly with the youth team, get them to a standard, then send them out on loan to help them progress in the hope that they would pay off, but of course they didn't.

I said to the manager that summer, 'Let's sell one of our big assets. I can take a bit of money and then the majority you can reinvest within the squad'. It was going to be one of the trinity at that stage. By selling one, it would allow Darren to bring in four or five players. I remember Barry at the time was worried that we were lacking, that we had no one who had previously played at this level before. But at that time we couldn't afford to bring in experienced players with the wages they were all expecting without selling one of our assets.

So I put the idea forward to the manager, and in hindsight now I think he regrets not doing it, because by doing so you give yourself a better footing. It sorts you out financially and gives you a better budget. But me being the chairman I am, I always support the manager. I will never sell anyone from under the gaffer's feet and Darren didn't want to sell anyone.

Maybe that was Darren's naivety and inexperience as a manager, and, although I pushed the desire to sell an asset, maybe it was my naivety as a young chairman that I didn't push the point enough.

I remember in all honesty it was George that I was trying to push for the most, but Darren loves the lad, so I was hitting my head against a brick wall on that one.

Nowadays Darren will tell you that if you need to sell a player, then you sell a player.

We had an OK pre-season, and then our travel to Pride Park to face Derby County was our induction into the Championship. I remember sitting in the directors' box and seeing about 30,000 people; it was unbelievable and a fantastic feeling.

We lost the match 2-1 but we certainly weren't outplayed, and we drew 1-1 against Sheffield Wednesday. West Brom came to our place and hammered us up until half time, going in at 3-0, we then brought it back to 3-2 and had two disallowed goals including a perfectly good goal by Aaron McLean. We lost away to Preston and then drew 1-1 at home to Crystal Palace, 1-1 with QPR, and 1-1 with Leicester City. These were in between beating Wycombe 4-0 and Ipswich Town 2-1 in the League cup.

We didn't look out of place at this level. I think the one thing that always seemed against us was luck. There were goals disallowed – Craig's against QPR, Aaron's against West Brom and Craig I think had another one at Derby. These were goals that shouldn't have been disallowed, and we could have been six or seven points better off. It's just about that little bit of luck that you need on your side at that level.

We played Reading and were 2-0 down at half time, but we stormed back with the trinity scoring to win 3-2. We then played Premier League Newcastle in the League cup at London Road, and if you look back it was probably the most dominant performance I have ever seen from a Peterborough United side. The football we played in that game was exquisite, and we won 2-0.

We went to Blackpool and lost 2-0, and then we had two home games on the trot, Plymouth on the Tuesday and Nottingham Forest on the Saturday. I remember flying out to New York, because at the time I was thinking about relocating there. The Plymouth game kicked off and at that point I was driving around the hills with Natalie and we were going in and out of signal, it was 0-0 and then we were in a black spot for about ten minutes. When we came out of that I had two texts in quick succession saying, 1-0 Plymouth, 2-0 Plymouth. I remember looking at

Natalie and saying, 'How are we losing to Plymouth at home?' It just wasn't going to plan; no disrespect to Plymouth but we shouldn't have been losing that game. We lost 2-1.

I remember speaking to the manager after the game, trying to gee him up. He was pretty low after that game. I flew in for the Forest match, and again we dominated the game and went 1-0 up. Then Joe Lewis gets injured and is replaced by James McKeown. I remember we should have gone 2-0 up and then suddenly because it was so windy, a shit cross that looked like it should have gone out into touch actually curled round James and went into the top right-hand corner. Three minutes after that they scored again. We lost 2-1. Losing those two games was a real bitter blow.

The manager felt changes needed to be made and to my surprise I was told that Andy Dibble was going to be sacked. This was a big deal: he was not only the club's goalkeeping coach, but he was one of the gaffer's best friends.

I remember Andy calling me in tears, he was in a very emotional state. I calmed him down and assured him that he was a good coach and that we would of course give him a good reference. Andy was in shock, he couldn't understand why he had been let go.

It turned out he later went on to Rotherham, and I still speak with Andy regularly now. He's a good guy, but I stood by the manager on his decision and told Darren to speak with Bob and get the contract sorted.

We drew the next game against Bristol City 1-1 and then I remember I was due to fly home after the Doncaster match. Doncaster scored three quick goals and blew us apart, we lost 3-1. Our naivety during that match really came to light.

I cancelled my flight home to have a summit meeting with the management team. I said, 'Guys, what do we need to do? Something's not right, we need to make changes.'

They said they were worried about the left-back position, so I said 'OK, who are we bringing in?'

And they couldn't find a good left-back, the only player they had on their radar was Scott Griffiths from Dagenham and Redbridge, but they weren't really sure about Scott. I said, 'Well OK, what do you want to do?' 'OK, we'll take Scott Griffiths,' they said.

No disrespect to Scott, but they just didn't know that much about the lad. I had mentioned Ryan Bennett previously. I spend a lot of time researching players and I knew that Grimsby fans absolutely loved their centre-half, Ryan Bennett. I mentioned the name to the gaffer, and Darren knew of Ryan but was conscious about the price tag on his head.

I remember saying to Barry, 'Barry, you're out of a job unless you do this Ryan Bennett deal!' He came back and said, 'Chairman, the Ryan Bennett deal is £500,000!'

I said, 'I don't care, just do it. He's nineteen years old, if the gaffer improves him and he comes good we could make £6 million on this lad. Just fucking pay it.'

So we did a deal with Grimsby, and in fairness to Ryan he didn't have an agent, he came in on his own and signed for peanuts. He didn't want big money, all Ryan wanted to do was play football and progress his career. We actually stole him from Scunthorpe, who had offered the same money, but we pipped them to the post through my urgency and pushing Barry to complete the deal.

Bennett and Griffiths arrived in the building together and were both available for selection for the Scunthorpe match, which we won 3-0. At this point we were twenty-first in the table on 11 points.

We then went to Blackburn in the League Cup. Again it was a match where all the decisions seemed to go against us. Joe Lewis got sent off and Russell Martin had probably one of the worst games he's had for us. We lost 5-2.

We then played Barnsley, a team that was in our pool. You always have a pool of teams that you look at that you can beat. Barnsley came to our place and we went 1-0 up, but Barnsley then scored two quick goals and it finished 2-1. We should never have lost that match.

FERGIE'S EXIT

Newcastle were coming up and we were struggling big time, and to top it off the relationship between me and the manager was deteriorating.

Before, we were so used to winning and talking, and when you're winning, having conversations all the time and keeping in touch is easy. But when you're losing, there is nothing much to talk about except that you're losing. Maybe my inexperience as a chairman told, maybe I didn't give him the support emotionally that I should have.

At that time I was in a bad place. I was dealing with so much crap off the field. The previous years all I had done was focus on the Posh, and I took my eye off my business, which cost me. At this point I was trying to concentrate more on my business, and I had to keep Posh as just a hobby as it were. This in turn led to the breakdown between the two of us.

Darren will tell you he couldn't handle losing. For the first time he started questioning his methods, the team a whole, and for the first time in our relationship, he was questioning my policy. He and his staff suddenly felt that these young and hungry players couldn't cut it in the championship.

He had never up until this point mentioned that he wanted more experience within the side, that had never been brought up. Now suddenly he wanted to bring in players on loan from the Premiership. All these players were on about £10,000 to £15,000 a week. We couldn't afford them. That was what I had been trying to explain to Darren in the summer, that by us selling a star player, that would have allowed us to purchase some experience.

Dean Keates, who had been our engine in midfield, suddenly struggled at this level. I remember Adam Pearson, who had had Keatesy many moons ago, tell me at the Derby game that Dean wouldn't be capable of playing at this level at his age. We needed someone in there pulling the strings alongside Paul Coutts, but without selling a big name we couldn't afford to do this.

I remember speaking to the gaffer ahead of the Newcastle game, and he told me he would be playing with one up front, which meant dropping Aaron. He was drastically changing our formation to cope with the opposition, which surprised me because Darren was always one who would play his way no matter what.

I popped to the hotel before the game and sat and had a conversation with the manager, and some of the things he was saying surprised me. He was naming players within the team who he felt weren't good enough for the Championship, and I said, 'Look, I think you're panicking, I think you need time.' We parted ways with a bit of a hug and then we made our way to St James Park.

Newcastle absolutely battered us. I think the only good thing to come out of the game was how well Ryan Bennett had performed. He had spent the day marking Andy Carroll and did a fine job. We lost 3-1 but I was more worried about the manager's mindset and demeanor, as opposed to the result.

The way it had always worked with myself and the manager is that at the end of a home match he would always come up and see me, and at the end of an away match I would always send a long text with my thoughts. If we won, it would be, 'Well done, maestro, blah, blah, blah,' and if we lost it would be, 'Fucking hell what happened there, blah, blah, blah' – he always likened it to war and peace. He would reply with, 'Cheers, Chairman, I'll ring you tonight,' and whether we won, lost or drew he would always ring *that* night.

That night I never sent a text to Darren. I felt it best I left it. I called Barry and asked him to speak with the gaffer, I said, I think he needs help mentally, and when people are under pressure it's easy to make decisions that are wrong. So I said to Barry, 'You need to calm him down and assess everything.' One thing I was always strong on getting was a defensive coach; I had pushed for this over the summer. Maybe now he would look to recruit one, as he could use the help.

I flew home the next morning and at this point Barry was due to meet with the manager. I said, 'OK, when you've finished, after the meeting, ring me and let me know how the manager's mind is.' I felt it best this was done by Barry rather than me because I didn't want Darren to think I was swamping him and putting him under too much pressure. I said, 'The one thing I ask is that once done and dusted, you get the manager to ring me for a talk.' Barry met with the manager, who told Barry that we needed to get rid of 90% of the squad. Barry said, 'Isn't that a bit drastic?' 'Nope, they're not good enough,' Darren replied.

With hindsight maybe he wasn't wrong, or maybe they were good enough but they just weren't getting any luck. I know you can only be unlucky for so long, but we really were unlucky. I remember Doncaster the year before had come into the Championship, they didn't win a game until Christmas, then they hit a good run and ended up finishing sixteenth. I just felt we needed to give it time, and with the manager saying this I took it as his cry for help, that he couldn't really deal with the situation.

I wasn't happy that he wanted to go in this direction and anyhow we couldn't afford to sell 90% of our squad; they were all on contracts, some on new four-year deals. Even players we had literally just brought in like 'Dave' were suddenly not good enough, and Charlie Lee, not good enough.

Three hours went by, no phone call. I rang Barry who was at David Gold's. I said, 'Barry, did you ask the gaffer to ring me?' He said, 'He hasn't rung you yet?' I said, 'No.' 'OK,' Barry said, 'I'll get him to call you.' Barry then called the gaffer and said, 'You gotta ring the chairman.' 'I will,' said Darren.

It got to 11 o'clock that night and still no phone call, and me being me, by this point I had got the hump. When you work for me, I expect *you* to ring me if I've asked you to. My wife said to me that night, 'why don't you just ring him?' I said, 'Honey, I'm the chairman, I'm his boss, he should be ringing me. I shouldn't have to be chasing the manager about.' And looking back, I was wrong. I let pride take over and I wish that I had just picked up the fucking phone, I really do, and just said, 'Hey, what's going on? Why haven't you rung me?'

It got to about two in the morning my time, which was 9pm UK time, and I rang Barry and said, 'He still hasn't fucking rung me!'

Barry was due to stay over at David Gold's that night, but in fairness to him, he left the party to go home and arrange a meeting with the manager.

He met with Darren the next morning and straight away Darren's body language suggested that he wasn't in a good place. Barry said, 'Why haven't you rung the manager?' to which Darren replied, 'He can fucking ring me!'

I think Barry suggested to him at the time that he had been tapped up, which Darren declined point blank. Barry said, 'Well, to have that response at a meeting like this, you must have another job lined up.' 'Don't be stupid!' replied Darren.

I then get a call from Barry saying, 'Look, he's not going to ring you, this was his response. What do you want to do?' I said, 'Well, by that response it says it all, he obviously doesn't want to be here anymore. Get on the phone and talk terms of compensation with him.' Within twenty minutes, the lawyer for the Ferguson family was on the phone trying to thrash out a compensation deal. It had gone all legal.

At this stage in my life my head was all over the place, and again I'll say I wish I had put pride to one side and picked up the phone. I had a newborn baby, many of my businesses were struggling, I was away working to try and save what little business I did have, working seven days a week, and my net wealth had decreased by 85%. This was to be the straw that broke the camel's back, as it were. So apologies to all Posh fans, because my attempts to save my business had a detrimental effect on the football club.

This was a dark, dark day. And me being me, the only thought in my head at that point was, 'Fuck him, he's gotta go!' And that was Darragh

MacAnthony talk: you challenge me, and I'm going to fucking eat you alive. I just wanted him out of my building. We paid Darren a year's wage in compensation and that was that.

We arranged a press conference to announce that Darren had left the football club. In hindsight maybe it wasn't such a great idea, maybe we should have just put a statement out and left it at that. Instead it turned into a circus. Maybe I should have done the conference on my own, but Barry being Barry wanted to sit up there with me and protect me from the media attacks I was about to experience.

The press conference started badly with a journalist having a pop at me, and without going into detail on what really happened, I was trying to explain it was a parting of the ways, it was mutual, and it wasn't one or the other. And Barry sprung to my defence and in doing so blurted out the now famous comment, 'He was tapped up!' Which of course was the wrong thing to say, and all hell broke loose.

As soon as the words left his lips I stood on his foot under the table. In my mind we had created enough palaver with this, I wanted it to go away, and this comment had done nothing except fuel the fire. I may be thinking it, he may be thinking it, but for fuck's sake don't say it! But now of course it was out there, and the only thing that was getting littered all over Sky Sports news was: 'Darren Ferguson was tapped up, claims Barry Fry.'

In fairness to Barry, he had said it to take the pressure away from me, and I felt sorry for him. Remember Barry has a mouth like me, and sometimes his mouth runs away from him and he says things he doesn't mean. And when all is said and done, as much as Darren didn't like what Barry said that day, and as much as he said it hurt him, Barry actually played a massive part in Darren getting the Preston job. The chairman at Preston spoke to Barry in length about Darren and Barry pushed hard for him to get the position there. I can't say I was a massive fan of that but I said to Barry, 'You just do what you gotta do.'

In all honesty, we have been very good to our former employees. Barry got Mark Cooper the Darlington job, he was also a massive part of Gary Johnson getting the Northampton job. I got Jim Gannon the Port Vale job. A lot of people don't see that; the press don't write about that sort of stuff. Football is a small world and what goes around comes around, so it pays for good managers not to fall out with their employers. In Darren's favour, he never really bad-mouthed me when he left. Cooper and Johnson both had a pop, but Darren was a model professional and I respect him for that.

I HAVE MADE A MESS OF THIS,
MAYBE IT'S TIME TO LEAVE

Suddenly I was left with a dilemma. I had just fired Peterborough United's most successful manager in recent history, Darren Ferguson, the son of Sir Alex Ferguson. I knew the media were going to absolutely destroy me. The manager had achieved back-to-back promotions and then, thirteen games into a new season, I'd sacked him. The fans were going to go ape shit, and all the blame was going to lie with me. I had to find a new manager quickly, and I had it in my head that I wanted to get it done and dusted in a day. I knew we were playing Sheffield United on the Saturday and I wanted everything in place for the visit to Bramell Lane.

I drew a list of names up: Eddie Howe, Jim Gannon, Andy Scott, Paul Tisdale, Pat Fenlon, and then Barry suggested Mark Cooper.

I really liked Pat Fenlon, he had an unbelievable record at Bohemians working with a young team on a tight budget; he ticked all the boxes. Then the weirdest thing happened: before Barry even had time to contact Pat, we received an email from an agency in Ireland with Pat Fenlon's CV on it. So I thought, Fucking hell, Pat Fenlon's the one!

We approached Brentford for Andy Scott, but they wanted silly money for him, something like £200,000. So he was a no go.

We spoke with Bournemouth about Eddie Howe, they didn't want Eddie to come; at the same time we had a phone call from Eddie's agent stating that Eddie wanted the move, so we were looking at ways to broker a deal with Bournemouth. Paul Tisdale didn't want to come, he wanted to stay loyal to Exeter. Jim Gannon was at Motherwell and didn't want to leave, so that was a dead end.

So meetings were arranged with Eddie Howe, Pat Fenlon and Mark Cooper. I also had David Oldfield and Dave Robertson apply internally from the club but obviously I felt it was too soon for them.

I actually asked Kevin Russell to stay on and manage the team but he refused, he actually left without compensation in loyalty to Darren.

I was excited to meet Eddie Howe, and I was excited to meet Pat Fenlon. When I flew in I received a message from Eddie Howe's camp saying thank you but no thank you, he was going all guns blazing with Bournemouth so no issues from me there.

I met Pat, spent time with him, and in honesty I was underwhelmed. For someone with his CV I was expecting a charismatic individual. He was a nice guy, but his agent was the biggest tit I've ever bet in my life.

I sat there and I had put together a document mapping out my time as owner, my policy, the players we had at the football club, the trinity, the youth system, etc., etc.

I was with Pat for most of the day, to the point where he actually stayed in a hotel overnight.

My big concern with Pat Fenlon was that he didn't know anything about the team, which surprised me. I'm a chairman and I can tell you all about the UK leagues, the Irish leagues, non-League, and I expect managers to be on a par with my knowledge at least. I also imagine that when people have interviews for jobs, they prepare, they find out about the company they are applying to and do their research, but with Pat there was none of that.

I explained to him the relationship I had had previously with Darren and he came back with, 'Well, don't expect a phone call or a visit from me after every game!'

So immediately I was getting the impression from him that 'it's my way or the highway' kind of thing, and 'my discussions with you will happen on my time'. Any manager will tell you that for success in a football club, there needs to be a good relationship between the manager and the chairman. They need to be in sync, and it was obvious that this was not going to be the case with Pat and me.

Pat went away overnight, and I still wanted him because of his record, but the more that time went on, the more my feelings towards the idea was negative. When Pat arrived the next morning, it was clear that he had done no homework, he hadn't watched the DVDs we sent away with him and he still didn't have a clue about our squad. He also made it clear that he wasn't going to come across with his family, which for me is a must for any manager. If you want a settled and dedicated manager, then you want his family to be around him for support, etc., and this wasn't going to be the case for Pat. It was as if he was saying: 'Well, let's see how it goes, then I'll move the family over.'

I didn't offer him the job, I said I had other people to see, but what I was doing with all the candidates was talking terms, so Barry, Pat and his agent went into the boardroom. Half an hour passed and Barry came into my office telling me that Pat wasn't a option, his agent was a waste of time and they wanted the king's ransom in wages. This turned out to be 50% more than Darren had been on, which was a lot of money, especially when this guy had only managed in Ireland and had never managed in the UK or at this level.

Had I have had a good feeling about Pat I would have fought harder with the negotiations, but I just told Barry to forget it and ask Pat to leave. His agent turned around and said that this was below Pat, we were being cheap and ridiculous.

A few hours later Barry received a call from Pat, who was at the airport, saying, 'Look, forget my agent, I want the job. Can I come back and talk to you?'

This wasn't for me. I told Barry to inform him that he could carry on getting on that plane. I think around that time Pat spoke with the press saying he had turned down the job for this that and the other reason, but I would take a lie detector test now to confirm all that I have just said.

Don't get me wrong about Pat Fenlon, the man has bags of potential and is obviously a top-notch coach. He's methodical, and without a doubt in my mind will go on to manage in England eventually and successfully. But it just wouldn't have worked out between us.

I spoke with two other managers, but for legal reasons these aren't worth going into to. I then sat with Kettering Town manager Mark Cooper and his assistant Nicky Eaden. People may laugh, but Mark Cooper interviewed exceptionally well. It was so good that it seemed rehearsed; he answered every single question exactly how I wanted them to be answered. It was almost like he had bugged the room from the last interview. It was perfect, almost too perfect.

He and Nicky sat and told us why we were struggling. The one thing Cooper was renowned for was keeping a tight defence; I know it was only Kettering, but that defence was a solid one. He was resilient at keeping to a tight budget, he knew our team inside out, he had watched a shitload of our games and his philosophy matched mine. He had done his research and wanted the job badly. He ticked all the boxes.

I had no other options and I was also needed back in the States to get back to work. I called a meeting with the players, and spoke with them as a group, and I couldn't get a word out of any of them; they were obviously in shock at Darren's departure, on top of the low self-esteem within the side due to our current League position.

I said to them that I felt the previous management team had stopped believing in them and that I was going to get a new manager in straight away. I said that I fully believed in them and that they could trust me fully. Looking back I expect I lost that trust and fucked up big time, but my intentions were always for the team, I wanted to do whatever was in my power to help them achieve success. But to many of them, I was the person who had just asked Daddy to leave home.

I offered Mark a four-year deal on the same money that Darren was on and he snapped it up with both hands. My only reservation was that he would be travelling from Birmingham each day. In hindsight maybe he knew that it wouldn't be a long-term position, who knows, but for me that wasn't the perfect situation.

Having Nicky Eaden as his Number 2 was a big plus for me. The guy had played at the top level for many years and it just so happened he was a defender, so obviously I felt that having a defensive coach as a Number 2, the defence would benefit hugely.

I knew the fans would be up in arms about the appointment but that didn't bother me because I had done it time and time again with players, and don't forget Darren came into the job on the back of no experience, so Cooper was already a step in front in my mind.

I stressed to Mark that it was important to get control of the dressing room quickly and get everyone on song, but it quickly became apparent that this wasn't happening.

Darren took some of the players out for dinner over the Christmas period after he left. When Barry told me about the meal situation I was livid, and I told Barry to contact Darren to tell him to back off. I remember saying to Mark, 'What are your thoughts on it? Because if someone had done that to me I would have made a point of getting in touch and telling him to fuck off!' But Mark didn't seem to have a problem with it. I expected Mark to react in the same way as I had, but he didn't seem bothered.

I then found out that Mark had brought his dad into training a few times which I thought was odd and the first player he wanted to bring in was Exodus Geohagen, who was a giant centre-back from Kettering. I wasn't happy with that, but I had to back my manager, he knew more about Ex than I did, and maybe he had a talent that I wasn't aware of. We also took a £10,000 punt on Josh Simpson from Histon.

The hangover from Darren was still apparent, however: the players seemed like they were pining over him. Aaron McLean, who was a big influence in the dressing room at the time, seemed to rebel against Mark for one reason or another, and instead of the dressing room picking up in spirit, it was dropping at the rate of knots.

We lost 1-0 to Sheffield United, then three draws followed: 2-2 with Middlesbrough, 2-2 with Swansea and 0-0 with Ipswich. We lost 3-2 to Coventry and then finally a win came about against Watford, winning 2-1.

The win was badly needed as we were still rock bottom of the Championship and maybe this would now install a bit of much needed confidence, but it wasn't to be the case.

We lost to West Brom 2-0 and our style of football had really dropped, we looked a beaten team before we had even kicked a ball.

My first full season, the League Two runners up 2007–2008 squad

League One runners up, the 2008–2009 squad

The calm before the storm, the 2009–2010 squad

Gary Johnson's 2010–2011 squad

Back together, the 2011–2012 squad

At Tranmere

Celebrating with Aaron McLean at Tranmere

Always happy to beat The Dons

Celebrating with the gaffer at Colchester after gaining promotion into the Championship (the first time around)

*Presented with a framed
picture of the ground
from Brian Mawhinney*

Me and my father at London Road

We then faced Cardiff City at home. We were 4-0 down at half time; the team got booed, and I was livid. I kicked the door off the hinges in my office and sat there contemplating whether to leave or not. Unbeknownst to me, Mark Cooper had gone and sat in his office and left the team on their own in the dressing room. I think he came back in with a couple of minutes left, made the changes and sent them on their way.

Rumours were circulating that I had called him into my office at half-time, which was absolute rubbish. At 4-0 down he wouldn't want to come anywhere near my office, believe me!

To be fair to the team on that day they came out fighting! Goals from Josh Simpson, Charlie Lee and George Boyd saw us end the game at 4-4, and I witnessed the greatest come back I have ever seen.

We then had a third-round FA Cup trip to Tottenham Hotspur and lost 4-0. The only thing that came good from that game was Joe Lewis' performance: he was sensational in that match, so much so that Spurs fans were even calling for him to be their Number 2! An International break was upon us, and I felt that the team needed to bond again to recreate the team spirit from the previous season, so I offered to pay for the whole squad to go off to Tenerife for a week. I remember the snow was bad in UK at that time, so training would also be improved for it. We had got some loan players in to help bolster the squad: Kerrea Gilbet, a right-back from Arsenal; Jake Livermore, a midfielder from Tottenham; Izale McLeod, a striker from Charlton; and Reuben Reid, another striker from West Brom. The trip would also give these players a great footing in joining the football club.

As it turned out I've heard that this was far from what I imagined it would be, and turned into more of a drinking fest than a football exercise. Paul Coutts wanted to leave the club and rejoin Darren, who was now manager at Preston; our new goalkeeping coach. Darren Ward, missed the flight to Tenerife purposefully in order to rejoin Darren – the place was falling to pieces.

We lost every single game in January, including the one match that I told Mark I needed him to win, Preston. I know Darren got a good reception from the fans, and it felt very strange knowing he was in the away dugout. I didn't make it over for that match because I didn't know how I would react myself. We lost the game 1-0. The final match that month ended 2-0 to Crystal Palace. I called Barry and I said, 'Look, I've made a mistake, I need to hold my hands up. You need to sack him.' So Barry sacked him. We had won one game in twelve, we looked shot and nothing like the team from last season. I gave Mark a good payout for his short stint and ended up having two managers on the wage bill for another year.

I supported Mark as much as I could but it was apparent that he wasn't ready for such a big job. What pisses me off is that he then came out in the Football League paper saying that the average wage at the club was £800 a week; he implied that I picked the team, etc., etc.; he really fed them a load of crap, and no one came to me asking for my side of events. I actually got Barry to call Mark and tell him that if he tried anything like that again I would hit him hard with a lawsuit!

I was pissed off because Barry actually got Mark the Darlington job, and their closeness annoyed me. I felt he needed to protect me better than letting shit like that come out that wasn't true.

I told Barry that we needed a problem solver. My mind was focused on Jim Gannon, so on the same day that Mark had been sacked I spoke with Jim and asked him if he could take over the side until the end of the season. I was very honest and upfront and explained that I couldn't afford another manager on a four-year deal.

Jim Gannon was a very methodical character. We would speak on the phone and each phone call would last for about two hours. Prior to his first match in charge he even sent me all the set plays and everything that was in place for that coming game. The attention to detail that he had was immense.

We won that match against QPR 1-0 and I felt comfortable at last that the team would be put back into shape. We lost 2-1 against Cardiff, 1-0 against Middlesbrough and then beat Ipswich 3-1 before ending the month on another loss, Swansea.

Jim had dropped Mackail-Smith and didn't see any importance in us keeping George Boyd. Nottingham Forest came in for George during the loan period, and Jim felt this would be a good move for the lad. Forest offered £50,000. I immediately said no. George had been our best players so far that season, and I wasn't about to add more woes to the side. I told Barry that the only way we would be letting George Leave would be to silly money. I said go back to Forest and say they can have him for £400,000. This was not a transfer fee, it was a loan fee, and an incredible amount for such a short period.

I was sitting in my office in Orlando when I received a call from Barry. He said, 'The Forest chairman wants to speak to you.' I said, 'Barry, you know I don't speak with other chairmen, that's what I employ you to do.' 'I know,' he said, 'but he wants to speak with you, they want to take George on loan for £400,000!'

I said, 'Are you serious? Barry, I was only joking when I said I wanted that much, I didn't actually expect them to come in with that kind of offer. I only said it because I thought they would come back by telling us to fuck off!'

I was devastated. Jim reacted by putting a seventeen-year-old in his place. It was no bother to Jim, that's how he works. I know he rubbed a few people up the wrong way but Jim Gannon is a very good manager. We actually still stay in touch to this day, and he did a bit of scouting work for us when in-between jobs.

Jim's philosophy was to create the club from the ground up: he loved the youth policy, and wanted to use that system as much as possible. If I were to buy a club from non-League, I would make Jim Gannon the director of football, because he would create one hell of a football club from the ground up.

I then got another call from Barry, who obviously wasn't very happy with how Craig was getting overlooked and isolated. I emailed Jim and asked why Craig was not in his plans and he replied by telling me that he didn't think Craig could hold the ball up, he couldn't head it, and overall he just wasn't good enough at this level.

He preferred someone like Liam Dickinson, who we actually brought in on loan. He was a big, tall, strong striker who could hold the ball up and wasn't scared to put his head in the firing line.

We then got our first back-to-back wins in the Championship against Sheffield United and Watford, Liam Dickinson actually grabbing the winner in the 1-0 win at Vicarage Road. But even that couldn't improve the form: we went on to lose the next five games on the trot. I remember going away on my wedding anniversary to Mexico, and getting off the plane to four texts in a row from Barry, all being goals to Scunthorpe. I had an email that evening from Jim saying he wouldn't be staying on at the club after the season.

So Jim was merely now filling a gap. We had shipped Boydy out on loan and now Craig was being dropped. The trinity was coming to an end and it hurt. At this point the only thing that was going through my head was that I had made a mess of this and maybe it was time to sell up and go.

I'm taking my son to Kung Fu one afternoon when the phone rings. It was Barry, and he said, 'Craig's in a hotel in Reading, what do you want me to do?' I said, 'What the fuck's he doing in a hotel in Reading?' 'Jim don't want him, he wants to bring in Will Hoskins, so this could be a great move for Craig,' Barry said.

I stepped out from the hall where my son was and said to Barry, 'Look, you get him out of that fucking hotel room and get him back to Peterborough. If he's not back in Peterborough by the end of the evening there will be hell to pay!'

Jim wasn't happy about this decision. I had stopped our star asset in my opinion leaving the club, and the rest is history.

I went away to Mexico, and I remember laying beside the pool and turning to Natalie and saying, 'I'm done with Posh.' I had completely fucked up our season, and I didn't have the money to get us out of League One. The clubs at that level were big hitters, it was a far stronger league than when we were last in it, and on top of that we would have the hangover from this season on us.

I now had to tell the public that Jim didn't want the job and I now had to find a new manager. What was I going to do?

I hadn't drunk vodka in years, but I found myself lying there drinking vodka and opening up to the wife. She kept saying, 'But you love Posh, you love owning a football club.' Maybe it was out of love that I contemplated walking away, maybe I didn't deserve to be at the helm of Peterborough United, maybe I had made one fuck up too many, maybe I had lost the fans' trust.

My ego at that point in my life wasn't good for taking criticism. The fans' message boards were slating my ownership and I actually got abused by one of our own fans at a home match, which for me, considering the time and money I had put into the place, made me think, Do you know what? I don't need this.

It was actually during the 4-4 game with Cardiff: some guy stood up, came over towards the directors' box shouting, 'This is a load of bollocks, why don't you fuck off back to Ireland?!' I was seconds away from dragging him over Peter Ridsdale and teaching him a lesson. Remember, my wife was sitting beside me during that match, and it scared her. The fact we were 4-0 down at that point didn't help, because I was already in a bad mood, but I just thought, after everything I have done for this football club, the millions I have pumped into it, taking it from the depths of League Two and putting it into the Championship and this is how I'm repaid? Really?

Everything at that point was going against me and I honestly couldn't see any light at the end of tunnel. I really was on the edge, and in all honesty it was Barry Fry that brought me back from the brink.

He would ring me and say, 'Come on, get your head up, its not your fault, stop feeling sorry for yourself!' And it was Barry who came to my rescue at that point with a manager. He called me one evening and said, 'Gary Johnson wants the job.'

GARY JOHNSON, RETURNING TO LEAGUE ONE AND COSTS SPIRAL OUT OF CONTROL

'Gary Johnson wants the job?' I said. 'We will never be able to afford Gary Johnson.' Gary had won god knows how many promotions in his time in management and had even managed the Latvian national team. He had recently been released from Bristol City, a team that the previous year he had got to the play-off finals. This was an experienced manager indeed, but at Bristol he would have been on around £700,000 a year. We couldn't afford that. Barry said, 'Well, let me have the conversation with him.' I said, 'OK, have that conversation.'

A day later Barry called and said, 'Gary wants to meet ya. It's not about the money with him, he's just had a big pay off. He just wants to get back into football.'

Out of all the names I had had, this was a good name. I had tried the inexperienced route, maybe it was time to go with experience. I said to Barry, 'OK, bring Gary out to Orlando and we can sit and discuss terms, etc.'

Jim was still in charge at this point, but I spoke to him about the situation and in fairness to him he was all for it. He felt Gary Johnson would be a great acquisition for the football club.

So Barry organised for the two of them and their wives to come out to Orlando. I picked them up from their hotel and we went to my office to meet and greet.

Gary was a funny guy, a joker and I've never met anyone in my life who can sell well, bar me, but Gary Johnson was a fucking unbelievable salesperson. He was the hardest negotiator I have ever been in a room with. I can negotiate with anyone, but this guy pushed me to the limits.

He had a figure that he wanted to be paid, and he did everything in his power to convince me to give him that money, which surprised me because originally it wasn't supposed to be about the money, and maybe that should have had the alarm bells ringing.

He spoke about formations, players, and it was agreed that we should sell some players, but then later on he had turned it round in his selling pitch that we should actually keep those players. Gary knows exactly what to say at the right time, he is a very clever man in that way.

We agreed on a wage that made him the highest paid manager we had ever had and this was in League One, which for that level was big, big money. The previous highest we had paid at that level was £180,000, so it was a big difference, but it was still nowhere near the figure Gary originally wanted.

He only wanted a two-year contract, and he wanted me to hire his brother as chief scout, which again should have rung warning bells for me. The club had never had a chief scout previously and in my opinion we didn't need one, especially one that was on such big money, but this was a deal-breaker for Gary.

I told Gary that money was limited and I made it clear that George Boyd had a year left on his contract and that he would need to be sold in the summer. Forest had decided that they didn't want George, so he had to go. Aaron McLean was another one; he wanted to leave and was becoming problematic. Gary said he would assess the team over the remaining four matches left that season and we would hold further discussions at that point.

Middlesbrough were bidding for George all through the summer, so we knew this was an option open to us. Gavin Strachan had gone back to his dad and said how skilful George was, and Middlesbrough came in strong for him. Unfortunately it wasn't anywhere near our valuation for him. I think they started at around £1 million with add-ons or something like that, but we knew that the coming summer George had to go.

Gary took charge for the Leicester game and we lost 2-1. Reading followed and we got smashed 6-0. From that result everything changed, suddenly from not having to spend any money, I was paying £70,000 on a new gym, £50,000 on refurbishing the changing room and putting new flooring down, £40,000 on modernising the physio room, it became ridiculous.

Gary informed me that cliques had been formed within the dressing room, people were separating into groups as opposed to being a team, which had gone a long way from our philosophy of being one big happy family.

George returned to training and suddenly Gary was ringing me every five minutes frothing at the mouth about George Boyd, and he was suddenly making a case for why we should keep George at the football club. This was the problem with Gary. We're not going to spend any money, so we buy a new gym. From having his brother and Number Two Nicky Eaden with him, he suddenly wants more money to bring Mark Robson in. So we now have a fucking huge backroom staff and a chief scout that we don't need. Then from selling George Boyd, to 'Let's keep George Boyd, Chairman, and we'll win the League'. We buy in his list of players, and then suddenly before we get on the plane for pre-season he wants two more... It was relentless.

We lost to Blackpool 1-0 and won our final game of the season away to Plymouth 2-1, and that was our season over. We finished the league rock bottom on 34 points winning only eight games from forty-six.

Our reputation with the press was now a joke. The club was more or less being portrayed as a caricature by the media and the football world collectively, I was seen as this guy that liked firing managers, and it all spiraled out of control. Sacking Darren, the most successful manager in our history and the son of Sir Alex, was like I had fired the son of god himself; it came back and slapped me in the face big time.

I hold myself completely responsible for the whole fiasco that took place that season. My biggest mistake was sacking Darren Ferguson, my second biggest mistake was hiring Mark Cooper.

THE LEAGUE TABLE

Pos	Name	P	W	D	L	F	A	W	D	L	F	A	GD	PTS
1	Newcastle	46	18	5	0	56	13	12	7	4	34	22	+55	102
2	WBA	46	16	3	4	48	21	10	10	3	41	27	+41	91
3	Nottm Forest	46	18	2	3	45	13	4	11	8	20	27	+25	79
4	Cardiff City	46	12	6	5	37	20	10	4	9	36	34	+19	76
5	Leicester City	46	13	6	4	40	18	8	7	8	21	27	+16	76
6	Blackpool	46	13	6	4	46	22	6	7	10	28	36	+16	70
7	Swansea City	46	10	10	3	21	12	7	8	8	19	25	+3	69
8	Sheffield Utd	46	12	8	3	37	20	5	6	12	25	35	+7	65
9	Reading	46	10	7	6	39	22	7	5	11	29	41	+5	63
10	Bristol City	46	10	10	3	38	34	5	8	10	18	31	-9	63
11	Middlesbrough	46	9	8	6	25	21	7	6	10	33	29	+8	62
12	Doncaster	46	9	7	7	32	29	6	8	9	27	29	+1	60
13	QPR	46	8	9	6	36	28	6	6	11	22	37	-7	57
14	Derby County	46	12	3	8	37	32	3	8	12	16	31	-10	56
15	Ipswich Town	46	8	11	4	24	23	4	9	10	26	38	-11	56
16	Watford	46	10	6	7	36	26	4	6	13	25	42	-7	54
17	Preston	46	9	10	4	35	26	4	5	14	23	47	-15	54
18	Barnsley	46	8	7	8	25	29	6	5	12	28	40	-16	54
19	Coventry City	46	8	9	6	27	29	5	6	12	20	35	-17	54
20	Scunthorpe	46	10	7	6	40	32	4	3	16	22	52	-22	52
21	Crystal Palace	46	8	5	10	24	27	6	12	5	26	26	-3	49
22	Sheffield Wed	46	8	6	9	30	31	3	8	12	19	38	-20	47
23	Plymouth	46	5	6	12	20	30	6	2	15	23	38	-25	41
24	Peterborough	46	6	5	12	32	37	2	5	16	14	43	-34	34

Now, although I was shelling out money that I didn't have, at least I had the promise from Gary Johnson that we would win the League at the first time of asking.

We flew out to Portugal that year for pre-season, and it was to be the first time that I would actually go along, travel and stay with the squad, so I was looking forward to it.

When we arrived I was horrified, the place was a dump. It was basically a pub with a load of apartments built on the side of it, no air-conditioning, and to top it off the place cost me more than La Cala did, which was a 5-star resort! I said to Gary, 'Why are you wasting my money on a shit hole like this?', and as normal he came back with the 'don't worry Chairman, I will get you your League title' bollocks.

I tried saying to Gary on many occasions, 'Look, do we really need this, do we really need that?' and he would always say, 'Look, you've got hundreds of millions, what are you worried about?' That used to wind me up like you wouldn't believe. Gary was often very condescending with me and it was like he would pay lip service but didn't really want my opinion or indeed value it.

For the first time in our recent history we were having to pay agents for all the players that were on Gary's list of targets and this didn't sit well with me. We paid well over six figures in agents' fees over this summer period. We bought striker Dave Hibbert on a free from Shrewsbury, and centre-half Kelvin Langmead for £80,000, also from Shrewsbury. I wasn't keen on these two signings, and didn't feel it was the direction we should be going in. Nothing personal against the two players but I didn't see any real future resale value in either of them, plus we were offering wages well above what they were already on, not to mention agents' payments again.

There was this Chelsea player that FC Twente apparently wanted; he was apparently the best left-back in the world, and would eventually generate the club millions. It was apparent on the first few days in Portugal that with Seth Nana Ofori-Twumasi we had wasted a three-year contract on a player that would struggle to get in our first eleven, never mind being able to sell him on for millions in the future as Pete Johnson kept telling me.

We brought in goalkeeper Steve Collis on a free from Bristol City, and I didn't rate him; midfielder Arron Davies on a free from Brighton, a player with potential but a poor injury record; Grant McCann was a real scoop and the best signing of the lot, on a free from Scunthorpe; and midfielder James Wesolowski from Leicester, a player that again had a poor injury record but looked like there was something about him. These were the players Gary and his brother wanted and as usual I backed my manager.

Jim Gannon actually had Grant McCann on his radar whilst at the club, and out of all the signings Gary had made, this was the one that I had confidence in. The rest I felt were strange signings and I knew that the majority of the players we already had in the squad, like your Lees, Whelpdales, Boydys, The Mac Attack, would be the ones to get us out of the League.

Whilst in Portugal I remember Charlie Lee playing out of his skin at left-back. He looked sharp, fit and in fine form, but Pete Johnson was like, 'Na, not good enough, Nana's a better player.' That wound me up from the sidelines during training camp not to mention the fact I found it odd that a scout had his own training kit and was actually out on the pitch at times.

Benno, whom we had just spent £500,000 on: 'Na, not good enough, Langmead is far better.' Barry and I were sitting there biting our fucking hands!

The Bennett comments had me reeling that summer before the season had even started. I just knew Benno wouldn't get a look in whilst Gary's player Langmead was in the building. That's £500k potentially down the fucking drain and potentially millions to us because I was convinced that's what the lad would be worth to us eventually. I actually fought tooth and nail to get Lee Tomlin into the club, he was a young exciting player that could play upfront or in midfield. He was signed to Rushden and Diamonds, a club that were struggling financially so much so that they eventually folded and went into administration. We had Tommo in on trial under Darren for two days but it was a period that Darren was off sick with the flu and Tommo was carrying an ankle injury.

When we came back from Portugal pre-season we played Rushden in a friendly and I remember saying to Gary and Pete that I wanted Lee Tomlin, I loved him. Pete would say, 'Well, he's overrated, he's not as good as he thinks he is.' Pete had a huge influence over Gary especially in the transfer department. Don't get me wrong, Pete was a nice enough guy, but he wasn't impressing me this far with his scouting work. I also didn't like the fact we were spending so much on agents fees. As I said before, this was the first time we had ever paid agent's fees, we must have spent high six figure fees on agents' that summer!

Lee Tomlin ended up coming to Posh as a trade-off, in order for Gary to get something. He wanted something and I said, 'Only if you buy Lee Tomlin', and that's how we snapped him up. For my money, that's one of the best £180,000 we have ever spent. We could sell Tommo tomorrow for £2 million! So I think my purchase has been justified. Barry also played a massive part in getting Tomlin here by actually forcing Gary and all his staff to watch a videotape of Lee tearing the Premier League side WBA apart in a friendly. Baz said, 'If you lot cannot make a player out of this lad, then you all need to depart football.'

Gary wanted George Boyd to stay, we had Middlesbrough on the table but Gary ground me down. Don't get me wrong, I love George Boyd, I always have, but it was time for him as a player to move on and time for us to cash in on our investment. In the end I signed George up to be the highest-paid player at the club, the highest-paid player in the history of Peterborough United. It was a mega three-year deal and one that had his agent reach for the pen and contract instantly. I guess the whole pre-season training period had got me all misty-eyed and dreaming of silverware and thinking with Boydy in our team that we were pretty much guaranteed to be in the reckoning.

I fought with Mackail-Smith to try and get him to sign a new deal, but he had a new agent and his agent was a complete prick. His agent actually gave me a message via Barry warning me away from actually talking money with Craig. My response to that was, 'Fuck you, he's my player, I pay his wages, I will talk with him about what I want!' I spoke with Craig in Portugal and he wouldn't sign a new deal, so we moved on. I knew Craig would play his heart out and not let this contract situation bother him or affect his play.

I know I have been pretty negative so far about Gary Johnson but this is all with hindsight, and hindsight is a beautiful thing. At the time, although frustrated with bits and bobs, I was actually excited by the prospect of the season ahead. I had got my mojo back and felt ready for the world of football again.

We started off the campaign in fine form, beating Bristol Rovers 3-0 at London Road, with Boyd, McLean and McCann grabbing the opening goals of the season. We then played Rotherham in the League Cup, winning 4-1. Everything was hunky dory.

We then went to Bournemouth, a team that had just been promoted from League Two. Ahead of the game the manager showed me the team and tactics for the game and told me that we would hammer Bournemouth off the park. We got tonked 5-1!

Gary blamed it on food poisoning and bad beds. I didn't, I blamed it on shit defending.

I didn't rate Nicky Eaden like Gary did, I didn't feel he could do this role for us or improve us where it was needed from a coaching point of view and those feelings kept circulating around in my mind.

We beat Huddersfield 4-2 after going 2-0 down, we beat Cardiff in the cup 2-1 and Plymouth 3-0, so the hammering by Bournemouth aside it was a good month. We were second in the league, one point from the top spot, and through to the next round of the League Cup.

And then the inconsistency began to set in. We lost at Tranmere, beat Oldham after going 2-0 down, drew at Exeter, lost at Swansea, beat MK Dons and finished September losing to Notts County at home, a game that got quite heated. McCann got sent off and at the end of the 90 minutes all hell broke loose between both sets of players and staff on the pitch in front of all the fans. They were disgraceful scenes.

We beat Carlisle 1-0, lost 3-2 to Huddersfield in the John Player Trophy, lost 2-0 at Hartlepool, got a topsy-turvy 5-4 win against Swindon. We lost 2-1 to Brentford and then we came to Brighton. This game Gary felt it necessary to badge up in the media as a Cup Final, no disrespect to Brighton but why would us playing them be a Cup Final? This gave us unnecessary pressure, I felt. So the game kicks off, Boydy does something stupid, gets sent off, and we lose 3-0.

After the game I got a phone call from Barry telling me that Bob had been told by the press officer that Gary had resigned at half time. He walked into the dressing room at half time and said to the players, 'You've let me down, I'm resigning!' He then sat for the remaining half and let his coaches take the game. I'm telling you right now that a sure way of losing the dressing room is to go and do what Gary Johnson did, because from that point onwards the players had lost all respect for their manager, so I have been told.

I couldn't believe what I was hearing. I got Barry to go and calm Gary down and get him back on board, I spoke to him that evening and gave him encouragement. It was my way of trying to support him. There was no way I was going to let Gary resign, it would have got twisted into it all being my fault and I wasn't having that. Gary told me that he felt he was under too much pressure and that he was letting me down, etc. I personally felt he was bottling it and trying to lay the blame at my door, cleverly.

It was plain to see pressure was getting to everyone. We were shit defensively, Kelvin Langmead was struggling big time at that level, we had conceded twenty-seven goals in the League alone up to that point and our star centre-halves Bennett and Zakuani were getting overlooked. Financially we were screwed: although Barry had offset things a little with the sales of Batty and Morgan by this time I was having to put up a £2 million overdraft at the club due to us being so much in the shit. Wages were starting to kill the club, Gary had spent a wedge and the gates had dropped. We were sitting fifth in the league, a large 9 points adrift of the top spot where I was expecting us to lie.

Rifts were starting to occur quite frequently between Gary and me, mainly over money. He wanted more players on loan with big wages, it was always a little bit more, a little bit more. I actually used to call him 'Give me more' Johnson. It was also coming to my attention that he wasn't spending a lot of time at the club, he was always going off to Bristol. It turned out that the house the club were renting for him in Peterborough was only being used by him, and his wife was still living away in Bristol.

All I kept thinking about at this point was that we were never going to get out of this League, it just wasn't happening for us for one reason or another.

We beat Walsall 3-1, drew against Stockport in the Cup, got absolutely smashed against Charlton, 5-1. We beat Stockport in the Cup replay 4-1 and I flew over for the Southampton game on the Saturday. Again we got mullered 4-1. We were conceding goals left right and centre, and Ryan Bennett still wasn't getting a chance. I decided I needed to act. That night I wrote an article in the local paper stating that I wanted us to win the next five games with no excuses!

I called a meeting ahead of the Leyton Orient game, and it was a very uncomfortable meeting. Gary sat there slumped with his arms folded and with his large team of coaches surrounding the table, and he made it very clear he didn't like my article in the paper. I made it clear that I wasn't happy with the defence and with how things were panning out.

I said, 'Look you've brought in Marcus Williams and Lewin Nyatanga, both on loan from Championship clubs, and they haven't performed but cost a fortune in wages. Adam Clayton we had in from Leeds, all these players on loan, why couldn't we play our own lads? Charlie Lee, Ryan Bennett and Chris Whelpdale.' 'You need to back me, Chairman,' he said.

'Back you?' I said. 'We've brought in all of these players and bar McCann and Tomlin the quality is poor. We are throwing money away on useless loan deals, we are falling down the League and conceding more goals than I'd like to mention, how have I not supported you?' And again he would say, 'What's a couple of million to you?'

I said there and then, 'Look, if we don't win the next five games, changes are going to happen whether you like it or not!'

We played Leyton Orient at home and drew 2-2, Aaron blew a penalty in time added on. After the match I said to Gary, 'Right, I want you to sack Nicky Eaden, he's not good enough.' Gary refused, he didn't like it. He stormed off home and Barry went on to fire Nicky Eaden.

Although this was something that Gary didn't like, he stayed on. We beat Bury 2-1 in the FA Cup and followed that up by beating Rochdale 2-1.

Hull City then came in with an offer for McLean and I turned it down. They then returned with a stronger offer, which worked out to be around £1.5 million. Aaron had been unhappy from the day Darren left the building, and as much as I loved Aaron he was becoming disruptive in the dressing room. He was making it clear he no longer wanted to stay at Posh.

In fairness to Aaron he put his head down for this season, scored his goals, was positive, and it all worked out for him. Gary of course understood and the sale went through. It was the end of an era, the Holy Trinity were no more, but I had to do what was best for the football club and the money from Aaron helped recoup some of the big money that I was spending that year.

I flew over for Christmas. Ahead of the Swindon game, I think it was like 23rd December, I went down to London Road for the day to take a look at the pitch, which is renowned for deteriorating at that time of year. I also felt it would be a good opportunity to have a good catch-up with the manager.

I went up to my office and about ten minutes later Gary came in. The first thing he said was, 'I've got twenty minutes for you before I have to head back to Bristol.' This shocked me massively. We sat for ten minutes discussing possible moves for Aaron McLean, then Gary made it clear he wanted us to spend £6,000 a week on a new striker. He wanted Danny Haynes from Bristol City or Aaron Wilbraham from MK Dons. I said to Gary, 'OK, look, I don't want to hold up much of your time, you get yourself off to Bristol.' After he'd gone, I turned to Barry and said, 'Fuck this!' By this time I had had more than enough of Gary Johnson.

I fly over from the States and this fella doesn't have the time of day for me in all honesty. His list of replacements for Aaron didn't fill me with confidence either to be honest and let's look at what they have done in terms of goal scoring since that day.

We played Walsall at home on 3rd January and by this time Darren Ferguson had been sacked by Preston. Clive Berlin came into my office. Clive is George Boyd's agent, and he also acts for Darren Ferguson. We were in my office having a coffee and Clive said, 'Why did you and Darren ever part company? Why don't you get in touch with him and have a coffee?' I said, 'Clive, I have a manager.' He looked at me, raised his eyebrows, I said, 'OK, I've got nothing against making peace with

Darren. Nothing to do with the Peterborough job, but on a personal level. But will he want to make peace with me?' 'I think so,' said Clive.

The conversation ended and nothing happened. We beat Walsall 4-1, and I remember lying in my bed one morning and looking at the League Table; we were eighth in the league, we had conceded more goals than anyone else, and I wasn't happy, I wasn't happy at all. My belief in us getting promotion wasn't there and to be honest I wasn't enjoying my relationship with Gary at all. I was spending money like it was water, players we had purchased weren't good enough, we had a £2 million deficit with the bank, and this guy was so inconsistent that we were never going to get out of this League, let alone win it.

We went to Fulham in the FA Cup, where we got spanked 6-2, and after the match I received a phone call from Barry saying, 'Look, Gary want us to send Ryan Bennett out on loan and he wants to sell Charlie Lee and Chris Whelpdale.' I said, 'Barry, none of these players have been given a chance. Bennett we invested £500,000 on and Charlie and Whelps had proven their quality at this level previously. No way is this going to happen.'

Kelvin Langmead was keeping Benno out of the team, a player that clearly was struggling at this level, but Gary refused to drop him for whatever reason. We had Brentford coming up on the Tuesday night, and given our League position, it was a must-win game for us. On the Monday word had come through to me that Gary was going to drop George Boyd for the Brentford game and of course play his favourite defender. I called Barry and I said, 'Fire Gary Johnson. I want him gone.' He said, 'What are you going to do?' I said, 'I don't know yet, leave that with me, just fire Gary Johnson, do a deal and get him out.' The whole 'Benno isn't good enough at this level and put him on the loan list' had made my mind up.

I was in Harrods that afternoon and I texted Clive saying, 'Is Darren up for that chat?' He replied back with, 'Name the place and the time.' I said, 'Tomorrow morning, my house in Ascot for breakfast.' Most people don't believe in going back. Fortunately I didn't take any notice of that popular opinion.

THE SECOND COMING OF FERGIE

I got home that evening and actually typed up a management contract for Darren on my home computer. I was suddenly all excited. The contract wages I set out for Darren were pretty shit: we couldn't afford hefty wages considering we were still paying for Mark Cooper and now Gary Johnson. But something just felt right, it felt like everything was happening for a reason and I couldn't wait for the morning to arrive.

My driver went to pick Darren up from Euston station at first light and brought him to my home in Ascot. He walked through the door, we hugged and we sat for ages laughing about the old days, speaking about our mistakes, apologising for those mistakes, saying how stupid we both were. He told me of his unhappiness at Preston and how he should have taken the Sheffield Wednesday job. It felt like old times, it really did. In all fairness I have never had that kind of comfortable closeness with any other manager, one where we could sit for hours yapping like a couple of old women (sorry, ladies). One of the first things Darren said was that he now believed and understood what I was all about, having now worked for other chairmen. He missed the interaction that we had together and how I would constantly spur him on. The chairmen he had had since barely spoke to him, whereas I never left him alone, and he realised that he needed that as a manager, that's how he worked best.

He appreciated the policy we had and realised that it wasn't about experience. I think when he was at Preston it was the experienced players that gave him a hard time and made his life difficult. In fact Darren's bad experiences were now good fortune for us. He was a changed character, and in those fifteen months away he had matured a hell of a lot. His wife was actually moving back to their former home in Stamford, regardless of Darren's involvement with Peterborough United.

He said, 'What's the contract?' I said, 'It's four and a half years and it grows with success, but at the moment I can only pay you pittance because of already paying for Gary Johnson.' 'No problem,' he said. He had agreed his pay-off with Preston, so he signed this deal without batting an eyelid, he didn't even involve his agent.

Another thing I love about Darren, is his lack of greed for money over his thirst for success as a manager. He is all about improving himself as an individual, a coach, and learning all the tricks of the trade to go to the top of the game.

We sat and discussed the direction that we wanted to take the football club. We spoke about the need to sell Craig Mackail-Smith, and possibly one or two more, we spoke about the youth policy and how I wanted to see our youth boys break into the first team as soon as possible, we spoke about the need for a training ground of our own, an academy, and we spoke about how we were going to get out of League One. It was all very positive and refreshing. My desire, hunger and belief was being reinstalled into me by the minute.

We had twenty-seven games left to play of the current season, and I think we needed to win seventeen or eighteen to gain automatic promotion. We knew it was a tall order, but Darren would have to get in there quickly and reenergise the troops.

He looked through all the papers of the club and saw the wages I was now paying players and he couldn't believe what he was seeing. His words to me were, 'Fucking hell, you've gone soft, Chairman, how has Gary Johnson persuaded you to spend all this money?' He knew that from what we had been paying previously to now was a big, big difference, and it needed to change and get pulled under control and quickly!

Darren knew that with the quality we had in our squad and the players we had onboard that we should be storming League One, but we needed to start getting some clean sheets under our belts, and to do this Ryan Bennett going back into the side was a must. Darren couldn't believe Ryan wasn't a permanent fixture in our side as he signed him and knew his pedigree inside out.

That evening we were playing Brentford at London Road. I had put the youth-team manager, David Oldfield, in charge of the team for that match, which didn't go down well with first-team coach Mark Robson, but I had known David for a long time and knew that he had no reference to Gary Johnson's motives or selections, whereas Mark, who had worked closely with Gary, may have gone down the same route as the previous regime. Plus at that point I wasn't even sure if Mark Robson would be staying or leaving with his former manager. So this was the best move at that time. I will say this about Mark Robson, we have never been the best of friends since he joined us but he is a top-class coach who knows what he is doing, improves players no end, and has a big future in the game eventually in management, which I know is his big desire. I know that had Gary have stayed for that match, George Boyd was going to be dropped. David Oldfield made a few changes, notably keeping George in the side and replacing Kelvin Langmead with Ryan Bennett.

I had made sure that no one knew about my meeting with Darren, and I invited him to the match as my guest, so you can imagine all the turning heads and the news circulating around the ground. It was pretty exciting stuff. We beat Brentford 2-1 thanks to a goal scored by Jonathan Obika, a kid we had on loan, in injury time.

We then decided we were going to do a big formal announcement so we announced a press conference for Darren's return the following day, and made sure that it was just the two of us. I think this disappointed Barry, but I felt it was best for that situation. Darren Ferguson was now officially the new manager of Peterborough United once more.

It was a very bold decision taking Darren back. People say never go back, but because of the way it had ended the first time around, and the animosity between both parties, to the outside it was something nobody ever saw coming. Keep in mind at this point I had just fired another manager, one with bags of experience, when we were only seventh in the league. So from people outside looking in, they must have been thinking, 'Jeez, what are you doing *again*!?'

So getting rid of Gary and replacing him with Darren was one of the bravest decisions I've had to make, but it felt right. When we reunited it was like it was meant to be. In fact it felt like I had handed over the keys of something I was holding, that I didn't trust anyone else with, and I was able to step away and go back to the States and continue in my life outside of Posh. It was a great sense of relief, if truth be told.

People have asked me since, had Darren not have been available, would I still have sacked Gary Johnson? The answer is yes, I would have. I didn't gel with him, I lost trust in the decisions he made, I was stressed about the financial plight of the club and I just cannot work in those circumstances. I certainly wouldn't have made the same mistake as last time, in rushing to replace him. David Oldfield and Dave Robertson would have taken the team for the remainder of the season, and time would have been spent in recruiting the best person for the job. I'm just grateful the best person for the job was available at that moment in time, Darren Ferguson.

The players that were present during Darren's first stint were very pleased to see his face, the lads that had joined previously were excited at the prospect of playing under Darren Ferguson, and I know for a fact that the fans were very pleased to see the messiah's return. As a side note we actually spoke about how, if we didn't go up automatically, could we go through the play-offs and make this a fairy-tale reunion at Old Trafford. Darren looked me in the eye and said without blinking, 'Chairman, if we end up at Old Trafford, we will not lose, and we will win, that I am certain of one hundred per cent.' My response was typical:

'Fuck that, I don't need the stress and drama of the play offs, let's go up automatically. Enough chit chat: let's make the magic happen again.'

MISSION IMPOSSIBLE

The good thing about having Darren back this time around was the fact that he wanted a close relationship with myself. He had had the shit kicked out of him at Preston and realised that having me as a chairman was not so bad after all.

I said to Darren that I couldn't give a fuck if we lost every game for the next three years as long as the club was working as one from top to bottom. I wanted him to work more closely with the youth set up of the squad and get them playing the same kind of football as the first team. I wanted players from the youth team breaking into the first team. I wanted new training facilities for our football to blossom. In honesty Darren was in a unique situation, he was in a job with no pressure.

I had a meeting with Darren fairly recently actually, where I asked him why some of youth players weren't getting the opportunity to break into the starting eleven. He said, 'There are one or two that are already good enough, but if I play them and we lose...' I said, 'Stop right there. We had an agreement from the off that that would not be an issue.' He said, 'But I know what you're like, if we lose six or seven on the bounce...' I said, 'Darren, that is not the case, I stand by my word.'

This showed him that my intentions were true. If we were going to be a proper football club, evolving, then we needed one or two youth lads breaking into our starting eleven each and every year. We would then be able to sell one of them each season for, say, £3 million, where that money would then get regenerated back into the football club and particularly into our youth development squad. This idea would invest more money into the youth system, give more money towards the wages of the first team and also give me some cash, reducing the debt owed to me. This, over a five-year period, would create a very good established Championship football club from top to bottom.

We again had discussions recently, in fact, that instead of us wasting money on loans, or paying money to bring in back-up, we should add our youth players to the squad as that back up. We should bring them up to a high standard where they would be ready to perform if called upon. Players like Peter Grant, who would be back-up to the centre-halves; Joe Newell, who is good enough to be in the first team; Kgosi, who would be backup to left-back; young Janaii, who is only sixteen years old, he's raw as you like, but the kid can be anything. So we have the groundwork done, and that's largely due to Darren's return to the football club. In fact since his return, six of the youth team members have been handed long-term pro deals.

With Darren back at the helm the football club was in very good hands, I was excited more than ever and now felt confident that promotion this season was ours if we wanted it.

Darren's first game in charge was as tough as it was going to get at that level, away at top-of-the-League Brighton. I remember that in the first half we were shit. Darren will tell you now that confidence in the side at that time was very low. In fact I think the team went into that game with no belief at all in being able to beat Brighton. The manager must have spoken some words of wisdom at half time because in the second half we absolutely battered them. We played the second half in our renowned diamond and Tomlin grabbed a goal back in the 66th minute. The match finished 3-1 with McCann getting sent off, to boot.

Hartlepool away was next, and this was like 'the return of Fergie'. It was our first clean sheet since 2nd October and we won the game 4-0. We went to Colchester and played them off the park and lost 2-1. We were now going into February, and at a vital point in the season. We were sixth in the league and 10 points from the top spot. I came back to England for the next two games which were massive, Sheffield Wednesday and Southampton, both at London Road.

We beat Sheffield Wednesday 5-3 in the kind of game that Posh fans have grown to get used to: we were 3-2 down at half time and then goals from Boyd, Mendez- Laing and Mackail-Smith sealed the win.

Southampton was much the same, we went 2-0 down early on and clawed it back to 2-2 at the stroke of half time with goals from Mackail-Smith and Whelpdale. We then lost two more shoddy goals to Southampton before McCann's converted penalty left us closing in for a point, then suddenly in injury time Tomlin calmly slots home yet another penalty and the game came to an end at 4-4.

After those highly entertaining matches I took Natalie off to Barbados for our wedding anniversary, and take it from me, there is nothing worse than waiting for Barry to text me with updates of matches. The Posh faced Charlton away, and the first text I received was to say we were 1-0 up thanks to Lee Tomlin, we went in 1-0 up at half time, we then came out and conceded three goals and Mackail-Smith pulled one back but it was too late, we lost 3-2. I remember Barry calling me explaining that he had never seen us dominate a match so much and when the final whistle went Chris Powell and his Charlton team were acting like they had just won the fucking FA Cup.

I spoke with the manager after the match and we had a good discussion. I explained that we needed to become consistent and put a nice little run together. I even put a little bonus in the air. I said, 'If we sneak an automatic place I will pay for the whole team to come out to the Bahamas to show my gratitude.' In fairness the gaffer felt very relaxed, he was very chilled. We were talking about the summer and we had drafted up a plan A and a plan B, Plan A if we made it into the Championship and Plan B if we stayed in League One. The latter didn't look at all pretty and basically involved us selling all of our big players, this was due to the projected budget in League One for the following season being 40% less than the season we were currently in, so we would have had to made drastic changes. But overall the talks were all very positive. I think what was refreshing, even after losing, was to hear the positivity in the gaffer's voice, and Barry drooling over our style of play, as opposed to previous regimes where the trust just wasn't in place. I lay by the pool feeling confident my club was in good hands and sailing in the right direction.

We went on to go eight games without a loss, winning seven of them. Five were clean sheets and included a 6-0 win over Carlise, 3-0 over Exeter and 5-0 over Oldham. It was true Fergie style. The diamond formation was working a treat and the gaffer had found a way to bring the best out of our skipper, Grant McCann, who was now one of our most consistent players. I remember talking to Barry and saying that playing this formation and style of football in the Championship would suite us down to the ground. I really fancied this to sit well at that level.

We went to MK Dons, a game that was to be televised on Sky, and I remember pundit Scott Minto speaking absolute bollocks about Craig, saying the only thing he lacked was pace! Was this guy serious? Craig is one of the quickest players I've ever seen, with a change of pace enough to cause any Premiership defence problems. It was obvious that Minto knew fuck all about him and clearly hadn't done his research on the guy. This irritated the hell out of me. We were banking big on Craig to go in the summer and this guy starts saying shit like that on live television with plenty of other higher-level managers tuned in.

Norwich City and QPR were both very interested in signing Craig. Neil Warnock, the boss of QPR, said that if they won promotion then Craig would be their Number One target, he was very interested. Norwich came in very strong near the end of the transfer window and unbeknownst to me Barry was up at Norwich negotiating a deal. The problem was that I had given Barry a price that I would accept for Craig to be sold, but that was way back in January. I appreciate people reading this may feel, why the hell didn't you know your director of football was sat at a boardroom table negotiating the sale of a player? However, understand that in football this is how it often works. But keep in mind *nobody* leaves without my final say so.

£1 million up front, with another £1 million in add-ons, was what I had originally quoted, but things had changed now. Craig was scoring goals for fun and looked like our fast-track out of League One. I remember thinking on this subject long and hard. Remember, financially we were fucked, so we needed this sale to happen, but on the other hand we needed to get out of this league and get back into the Championship. I also wasn't prepared to let him go for less than his worth, which to me was going up every day. He would possibly win the golden boot, win Player of the Year and get a lot more headlines through the end of the season, so the Norwich offer was now not so exciting.

Barry rang me from Carrow Road and explained that Norwich had met the asking price for Craig and what did I want to do? I was shocked that Barry was actually at Carrow Road in the first place, and the news he was giving me was not sitting right with me. Darren was back on board, we were gathering momentum, Craig was a massive part of that, plus there were only a few games left of the season. Barry's argument was that his contract was nearing an end and what if he was to get injured? Barry also felt that if we didn't go up, or if Craig lost form, then this kind of offer wouldn't happen again. I actually said to Barry, 'Baz I honestly feel we could get £3 million for the lad in the summer. Also I need to chat with the gaffer for his opinion as well, so let me come back to you.' Norwich also offered us Simeon Jackson on loan with them paying all his wages till the end of the season. We had chased this lad twice previously and I knew the gaffer fancied him big time, but timing just wasn't right to maybe bed in a new player. Ironically enough, Craig scored the goals to get us promoted and Simeon actually got back in Norwich's first eleven and scored a boatload of goals to get them promoted. That is football.

I called the gaffer and said, 'Look, Norwich are in for Craig.' 'How much?' he asked. '£1 million plus add-ons' I said. 'Too cheap,' he said, 'and at this stage of the season we need him.' I said, 'But we need the money.' 'Look,' he said, 'if you need the money, take the money.' I said 'OK, we'll keep Craig until the end of the season and he can score the goals to get us promoted.' This was obviously music to the gaffer's ears. I know Barry wasn't happy; he felt that I had moved the goal posts, and we had a bit of a row over this, in fact. I had to remind him who his boss was and where his loyalties lay. I said, 'Barry, at the end of the day you work for me, not Craig, not his agent, *me*! We are not selling Craig

Mackail-Smith to Norwich. If they want him in the summer, happy days, but Craig is not leaving London Road until that point at the earliest.'

Norwich threw a hissy fit at that response, but we had every right to decline their offer. Yes, they were going for promotion, but so were we, and we were in a better position with Craig in our corner than not having him there at all. McNally, their Chief Executive at Norwich, took a disliking to this and obviously has had the odd pop at us and Barry since. He wasn't exactly easy to deal with when we tried to buy Cody McDonald from them later on that summer, which is disappointing, but in all fairness I didn't even know Barry was at Carrow Road. Had I known he was going there I would have put the price up to save all this fucking about. Anyhow, since then we have done business with them again and I think all is well, so no harm, no foul.

Craig took the news pretty well, in fairness to him. He's that sort of character, though, he just wants to play football. The gaffer had a talk with him and asked him to get his head down and score goals and wait for a big move in the summer, which is exactly what he did: the lad is a model professional.

Barry was in a very difficult situation. Craig is in a long-term relationship with Barry's daughter and this kind of move would change Craig's life for the better financially and would see him in the Premier League, so I felt very sorry for Barry. However, when I reminded him of his position he said his loyalty lay with the football club, and I give him that, it all calmed down and we waited until the end of the season. Barry gets a lot of stick at the best of times but there is nobody better at the job he does, trust me on that.

It's all about margins, and this particular margin had our season hanging in the balance. Would we have been promoted had Craig not stayed? I don't think so.

It wasn't long after actually that Craig was called up to the senior Scotland squad, and has become a regular since, but that was on the back of the incredible season that he was having for Peterborough United.

Back to MK Dons: we lost 1-0, but again we created the most chances and played the better football. However, it wasn't to be. We then created another little run of five games without loss; we were now fourth in the league on 74 points. We lost against Leyton Orient 2-1, and at that point we all started thinking of the play-offs.

The play-off final this year for League One was due to be held at Old Trafford, home of Manchester United. Barry had always told me that the best way to get promoted was through the play-offs. It sounds great, because you have a lovely Cup Final game in a lovely ground, generate a bit of money, etc., etc., but one slip-up and that's your whole season unravelled in an instant. Again, the margins are that fine.

We drew with Yeovil 2-2, drew with Rochdale 2-2 and beat Dagenham at home on the final game of the season 5-0. We were fourth in the table at the close of play on 79 points.

The financial side of the football club at this stage was fucked: we were something like £4 million over our budget, and the bank overdraft stood at £2.2 million, which I'm on the hook for. As I mentioned before, if we were to stay in League One then the budget for the following season would be 40% less. I was absolutely shitting myself because how the fuck would we survive? OK, the sale of Craig would help, but we were still going to be short. Don't get me wrong, we certainly weren't going to be going into administration, but we would have to be clever in selling our best players and also look into ways of resolving the situation without showing panic to the world.

I had put in around £10 million at this point in total since taking over the club, and I wanted the club to become more self-sufficient. Through selling big names, the club would get a huge portion, and I would get a chunk reducing the debt. I remember that when Aaron was sold in December I took £300,000 from the sale, only to be called six weeks later asking for it back to put into the club, due to again needing to bring another player in. So the whole play-off experience, a lottery if you will, was upon us and it was a genuinely scary time. I had reached the end, or rather the mental limit, of myself putting money into the football club: it was now time to make the football club work as a business, and the first step was to win these play-offs.

THE LEAGUE TABLE AT THE END OF THE SEASON

Pos	Team	P	W	D	L	GF	GA	GD	PTS
1	Brighton & Hove Albion (C) (P)	46	28	11	7	85	40	+45	95
2	Southampton (P)	46	28	8	10	86	38	+48	92
3	Huddersfield Town	46	25	12	9	77	48	+29	87
4	Peterborough United (P)	46	23	10	13	106	75	+31	79
5	Milton Keynes Dons	46	23	8	15	67	60	+7	77
6	Bournemouth	46	19	14	13	75	54	+21	71
7	Leyton Orient	46	19	13	14	71	62	+9	70
8	Exeter City	46	20	10	16	66	73	−7	70
9	Rochdale	46	18	14	14	63	55	+8	68
10	Colchester United	46	16	14	16	57	63	−6	62
11	Brentford	46	17	10	19	55	62	−7	61
12	Carlisle United	46	16	11	19	60	62	−2	59
13	Charlton Athletic	46	15	14	17	62	66	−4	59
14	Yeovil Town	46	16	11	19	56	66	−10	59
15	Sheffield Wednesday	46	16	10	20	67	67	0	58
16	Hartlepool United	46	15	12	19	47	65	−18	57
17	Tranmere Rovers	46	15	11	20	53	60	−7	56
18	Oldham Athletic	46	13	17	16	53	62	−9	56
19	Notts County	46	14	8	24	46	60	−14	50
20	Walsall	46	12	12	22	56	75	−19	48
21	Dagenham & Redbridge (R)	46	12	11	23	52	70	−18	47
22	Bristol Rovers (R)	46	11	12	23	48	82	−34	45
23	Plymouth Argyle (R)	46	15	7	24	51	74	−23	42
24	Swindon Town (R)	46	9	14	23	50	72	−22	41

With us finishing fourth and MK Dons finishing fifth the two of us would meet in the play-off semi-final. I'm superstitious, and MK Dons were like our fucking nemesis, and if anyone was going to fuck us over it would be them. The first leg was at Stadium MK and in honesty I was pretty chilled.

For these play-off games I will include the official match reports from the day which were up on www.theposh.com. This is the best way to describe the highs and the lows of each match.

THE PLAY-OFFS

They say nothing is won and lost in the first leg of a play-off and that is true of this entertaining encounter at Stadium MK, which included two sending offs, five goals and an uncomfortable amount of injuries for Darren Ferguson's men to contend with. Posh lost Charlie Lee to a second booking, while Stephen Gleeson was dismissed for the Dons, as Posh threw away a 1-0 lead to find themselves 3-1 down before a composed penalty from Grant McCann kept the tie alive.

Milton Keynes Dons got the game underway, kicking towards the masses of Peterborough United supporters behind Joe Lewis's goal, with over 4,300 officially backing the boys in blue. Within the first few minutes, Posh were dealt a huge injury scare as Charlie Lee and Joe Lewis collided as the former cleared the danger after a slick one-two between Sam Baldock and Daniel Powell.

Both players were left in a heap on the floor and with the problems the club have experienced at left-back, the state of Lee would be a major concern. Thankfully both players were back on their feet, although Lee looked in pain as he walked over to the sidelines. It was all smiles on nine minutes as the deadlock was broken as a shot from Nathaniel Mendez-Laing was parried by goalkeeper David Martin into the path of Craig Mackail-Smith who made no mistake. A snap shot from George Boyd was gathered cleanly by Martin on the quarter-hour mark as Posh continued to dominate in the early exchanges. Mackail-Smith then fired over with his left foot after excellent approach play from Charlie Lee and Mendez-Laing. Lee Tomlin was denied by Martin after an initial error from the goalkeeper with his distribution on 27 minutes, in fact as it stands, the only concern for Posh was the fitness of Lewis who was signalling to the bench he was in trouble.

Baldock was inches away from converting an Angelo Balanta cross at the near post moments later, but he failed to get a touch to the low driven cross. Posh were then dealt another blow as Zakuani sustained a shoulder injury, with Kelvin Langmead replacing him. Stephen Gleeson sent a 20-yard shot wide of the target, while Posh were down to 10 men. As the first half entered the final minutes, the home side were on top, retaining good possession and goalkeeper Lewis, appearing to be only 50 per cent fit, made a stunning stop from close-range to deny Doumbe's header. Powell then saw a 20-yard shot deflected over the crossbar by Kelvin Langmead and Posh were sitting very deep as the Dons pressed.

I remember going out for a cigarette and thinking how well it was going to plan, maybe even too well.

Posh were dealt a blow at the interval as goalkeeper Lewis was forced off with former Exeter City shot-stopper Paul Jones in between the sticks for the second period. Jones had a nightmare first minute as he fumbled a header back across goal by Rowe and Powell bundled the ball over the line. The goal came less than a minute after the re-start. Boyd immediately fired wide of the near post after a good move involving Mendez-Laing, but Posh need to clear their heads at the back as the Dons have come out fired up. They couldn't and the Dons had turned this game on its head within five minutes of the second half as Sam Baldock fired an unstoppable 25-yard shot into the bottom corner after Rowe was penalised for a foul.

Lee was mysteriously booked for appearing to win the ball from Powell on 55 minutes and it was all one-way traffic now as the Dons, buoyed from their early strikes, took the game to Darren Ferguson's men. Powell somehow missed a header at the back post when well placed before the Dons made it 3-1 as Balanta cut inside from the left and fired low past Jones and this was a nightmare second half. Baldock then curled inches over the crossbar as the rampant Dons went for a fourth, attempting to put this tie to bed before the second leg.

Ferguson introduced David Ball from the bench to replace Mendez-Laing on the hour mark. Posh were inches away from reducing the arrears at the other end as Bennett, Ball and Mackail-Smith were all denied, one from the goal-line, after Martin struggled to deal with an in-swinging corner from McCann. The day went from bad to worse on 67 minutes as Lee received a second caution for a foul after Langmead's shocker of a pass put the left-back in all sorts of problems. Posh will point at the first booking, which was contentious as he appeared to win the ball. It was inches away from a deserved fourth on 69 minutes as Baldock found room in the box, but he curled the ball narrowly past the post. Substitute Ball was inches away from scoring a wonderful individual effort on 72 minutes, he dragged his right-foot shot just past the far post. The Dons were reduced to 10 men moments later as Gleeson was shown a straight red card for bringing down Little who had beaten three defenders and burst into the box. Captain McCann stepped up and converted from the spot – admirable bottle to send the goalkeeper the wrong way.

The goal got the Posh fans going behind the goal, knowing that a one-goal deficit to take to London Road, given the amount of injuries sustained and the problems encountered along the way, would be a commendable achievement. Mackail-Smith was inches away from an equaliser on 88 minutes, but his low 20-yard effort flew just past the post with Martin stranded. Four minutes of stoppage time was indicated by the fourth official, in truth, both teams would probably be happy with that. Paul Jones parried a Doumbe shot in stoppage time as both sides belied that statement of settling for the scoreline.

Final Score: Milton Keynes Dons 3-2 Posh

MK Dons: Martin, Lewington, Doumbe, Mackenzie, Gleeson, Baldock, Clayton, Balanta (sub Ibehre 79min), Chadwick, Powell (sub Marsh-Brown 77min). Unused subs: Guy, Searle, Woodards, G. Baldock, Chicksen.

Posh: Lewis (sub Jones 46min), Little, Lee, Zakuani (sub Langmead 31min), Bennett, McCann, Rowe, Tomlin, Boyd, Mackail-Smith,

Mendez-Laing (sub Ball 60min). Unused subs: Whelpdale, Davies, Newell, Wesolowski.

Attendance: 12,662

The fact that we had lost our best goalkeeper, our best centre-half, and we had our left-back sent off, no one ever speaks about those bits. Bitter MK fans will say we had a penalty that should never have been given, but then they forget that when that foul was made, the ball rolled to Boydy, who put the ball in the back of the net anyway, so regardless of the penalty we still would have scored at that point.

At the point MK were 3-1 up I was in complete shock, they were at us non-stop. Fortunately for us, Baldock missed a sitter which would have made it 4-1. Suddenly Karl Robinson, the manager of MK, looked to settle for the current result: they changed their formation and made a couple of subs. Our gaffer smelt the blood in the water and made sure that our fullbacks bombed on regardless of only now having ten men. Mark Little made one of his trademark runs, we don't know what he's doing, the fans don't know what his doing, he doesn't fucking know what he's doing and suddenly he gets in the box and goes down. Penalty Posh.

Pete Winkleman, who I love, was irritating the fuck out of me. He had seen the decision again on the TV and was running around the directors' box like a headless chicken saying, 'It's not fair, it's not fair.' He then ran down to the tunnel area and was leaning over the touchline shouting, 'It was never a penalty.' As I said, I have a lot of time for Pete, but this was something that he shouldn't have done. I mean, look at some of the decisions we have had at Posh over the years. OK, I get angry and raise my voice, but I would never run down to the technical area showing myself up. Never.

At 3-1 down I was telling Barry I was getting a flight home that evening back to America, I was done, I'd had enough. Then Captain Cool, Grant McCann, slotting home the penalty under massive pressure, suddenly put us in a good position. We were 3-2 down going into the next leg, at a sure-to-be packed London Road, and everyone who knows Posh will tell you that we love being under pressure at London Road. I left Stadium MK in a foul mood, and returned back to my home in Ascot pondering on absolutely everything, the situation we were in financially, the fact we were a goal down going into the second leg, everything. The calmest person that week was Barry Fry. I remember he called myself and the gaffer on many occasions saying, 'Calm the fuck down, its 3-2, it's over two legs, we're at home, it's gonna be a fucking sell out, we can do this!' Remember, Barry had been there, done that; he was the most experienced person out of the lot of us.

Everyone connected to Peterborough United pulled together during this period. I remember writing to the players a letter ahead of the first leg, thanking them for their efforts this season, and to try and give it one last big push. Joan Hill, who was the Player Liaison Officer, was gravely ill at the time, and I asked them to win the game for her, do it for Joan. The letter apparently brought a tear to a few players' eyes. When we lost, I thought it was due to me putting everyone on a downer.

Neil Gilby, who is the man behind Peterborough United TV, PoshLive, and the guy that helped me write this very book, had actually put a video together over a piece of music that the gaffer had suggested, Adele's One and Only. The video put to that song was incredible, it featured clips of each player, stunning goals, the play-off trophy – it had the lot, and it was so inspirational. I remember when I watched it, it made the hairs on the back of my neck stand up. I have since been told that the players watched this in the dressing room ten minutes from kick off ahead of both the second leg and the final. The players all put their arms around each other and watched it. Players and the manager will talk to you about it now, and how much it inspired them, so much so that the team's entrance music at London Road for the 2011/12 season was to be that very song.

The day of the second leg, I remember the atmosphere was unbelievable. We had a full house, and I did a lap around the ground signing autographs and applauding the fans for their support. It turned out to be one of the most exciting, electric and satisfying nights of my life.

Peterborough United booked their place in the League One final at Old Trafford after a superb 2-0 victory over Milton Keynes Dons at London Road. In front of a sold-out home crowd, this second leg of the play-offs got underway in lovely summer sunshine with a cracking atmosphere inside the stadium. Posh had an early chance as Tommy Rowe found Craig Mackail-Smith, but from a tight angle, his shot was pushed around the post by goalkeeper David Martin.

It was first blood to the boys in blue and the tie was all square as skipper Grant McCann curled home a free-kick past Martin at his near post to send London Road into delirium. At the other end, goalkeeper Paul Jones pushed a Daniel Powell shot around the post and it was a save that will make him feel very good about himself, coming so early in proceedings. The visitors were winning plenty of corner kicks and from the third successive flag kick, centre back Gary Mackenzie glanced an effort wide of the target.

Jones did well with the previous set-pieces to punch clear. James Wesolowski saw a shot blocked after letting fly from a distance on 27 minutes and it was a tense atmosphere inside the stadium with both sets of fans displaying signs of nerves. Moments later and Posh were inches away from making it 2-0 as a superb burst down the left from Grant Basey saw him reach the byline and deliver a cross that somehow managed to elude both Mackail-Smith and Tomlin sliding in.

A snap shot from Mackail-Smith, again from a tight angle, was pushed away by Martin after excellent work in the build-up from Tomlin. Mackail-Smith then saw a header deflected behind for a corner kick. The Dons struck the woodwork on 37 minutes as Baldock sent a volley crashing against the underside of the bar before the ball was hacked away and then a foul on Bennett relieved the panic. A McCann effort was then deflected goalwards by Boyd, but Martin made a sharp stop, diving to his left. Tomlin was cautioned four minutes into the second half for a foul on the halfway line. Half-time: Posh 1-0 Milton Keynes Dons.

Tomlin sent a left-foot shot wide of the target moments after the re-start as Posh tried to find that second goal early in the second period. Chadwick was then cautioned for a foul on Tomlin. Posh got the second goal of the game on 54 minutes and it was fitting that Craig Mackail-Smith found the back of the net, albeit at the second attempt after his shot had been blocked following a fine save from Martin to deny Boyd. Posh had the ball in the back of the net on 59 minutes as Tomlin rifled home, but the referee called it back for a foul to the dismay of the home fans and the player himself, who was left in a heap on the floor.

James Wesolowski produced a stunning last gasp tackle to deny Chadwick moments later as Dons countered at pace following McCann's free-kick which struck the wall. Posh were dealt a further blow on 68 minutes as skipper McCann went down for treatment on what looked like a hamstring injury. Chris Whelpdale replaced him in midfield. Tommy Rowe was superbly denied by the legs of Mackenzie after good work from Whelpdale down the right – this third goal was proving elusive for the boys in blue. Lewington was booked for a blatant push on Whelpdale, sending him crashing into the advertising boards. Gleeson and Marsh-Brown were so annoyed by the way things were going that they started on each other and bizarrely the referee got involved and called both players towards him to calm things down. Dons skipper Lewington nearly scored an own-goal on 85 minutes as his header was tipped over by Martin after a deep Basey centre. Lewis Guy replaced Sean O'Hanlon in a bold move five minutes from time.

Moments later and Posh struck the woodwork as Mackail-Smith robbed Mackenzie and bore down on goal, but his shot was pushed onto the post by the impressive Martin. Whelpdale then drove inches past the post as he raced clear and if Posh don't win this, they will point to so many missed chances in front of goal. Five minutes of stoppage time was indicated by the fourth official as Posh piled forward.

Final Score: Posh 2-0 Milton Keynes Dons, Posh win 4-3 on aggregate

Posh: Jones, Little, Zakuani, Wesolowski, Boyd, McCann (sub Whelpdale 70min), Mackail-Smith, Rowe, Bennett, Tomlin, Basey. Unused subs: Richardson, Langmead, Ball, Mendez-Laing, Davies, Newell.

MK Dons: Martin, Lewington, Doumbe, Mackenzie, O'Hanlon (sub Guy 86min), Gleeson, Baldock, Balanta, Clayton, Chadwick (sub Ibehre 65min), Powell (sub Marsh-Brown 65min). Unused subs: Searle, Woodards, G. Baldock, Chicksen.

Attendance: 11,920 (2,005 Dons fans)

The match was incredible. I can't even remember MK having a shot on target, we were that good from start to finish. Again we missed bags of opportunities, and Tomlin scored a great goal that was disallowed.

Throughout the whole 90 minutes I sat silently. I didn't cheer, I didn't react, I just sat there, my body was killing me and I was struggling to breathe. The relief when the final whistle went was a feeling that I find impossible to describe.

We celebrated like we had won the Champions League, we were that thrilled to come from behind and do it so convincingly. We were now bound for Old Trafford to meet Huddersfield in the final, who had beaten Bournemouth to get to that stage. The fans came onto the pitch, I got dragged into the changing room and we then went up onto the balcony to celebrate with the fans. It was a moment that will stay in my memory until the day I die. I spoke with the gaffer after the match and all he kept saying was, 'We're gonna win at Old Trafford.' I said, 'Don't forget you're in the away dressing room.' He said, 'I couldn't give a fuck, we're gonna win at Old Trafford.' He was that convinced, to him it was a certainty.

The time between the second leg and the final was something like ten fucking days, it was the longest wait of my life. Everything was to come down to 90 minutes of football at the home of Manchester United. The one thing I didn't want was for it to go to penalties. I didn't want us to lose on penalties and I didn't want them to lose on penalties, I just don't think it's fair. I would rather it be battled out in 90 minutes, the old-fashioned way. This whole season was to rest on the balance of one match, and for it to go to penalties would mean that all it would take is for one person's goolies to shrivel up and you'd be fucked, and that would be the end of that.

I flew in the morning before the big day, and drove from London to Manchester with Natalie. We arrived at the team hotel in Worsley at around 11 o'clock. As we entered the hotel, the manager and players were in the lobby ready to leave for training at Manchester United's training complex in Carrington. I remember the manager was so calm and collected, he came over and said, 'Do you want to play golf with us at 2.30?' I said, 'Golf? I couldn't hold a fucking golf club at a time like this. I'm a fucking nervous wreck!'

I decided it be a good idea to put my head down for a few hours. Natalie knew I was in turmoil. I arose at around five in the evening and went and got some dinner. I went through to the room that was booked for the club, and the team and management were all in there waiting for the Champions League final to begin between Manchester United and Barcelona. I had some grub and then the manager, who had been sitting with his management team, came over and sat with me to watch the game. This is something he would never have done the last time round.

Being in there, and seeing the likes of Tommy Rowe walking around in his flip-flops, Lee Tomlin joking with team mates whilst munching on a salad, everyone seemed so relaxed. I know that a group of the lads had been to Old Trafford that afternoon to watch Stevenage in the League Two Play-off Final, so everyone was just getting on with it, which was great.

The day before, I know the team went to Old Trafford themselves to take in the sights, walk on the pitch and to take a look at their dressing room. This is something Huddersfield chose not to do for whatever reason, but I felt it was a good idea for them to try and get used to their surroundings.

Unfortunately for the gaffer Manchester United lost in the final of the Champions League. Before the final whistle, the gaffer had retired for the evening to spare the jibes from Lee Tomlin, I'd imagine, who was the only person in the room supporting Barcelona. I had a Chinese on returning back to my room and slept like a baby.

When I woke the next morning I took a shower, and got dressed into my suit. Natalie's dad came up with her brother and we met up to have some breakfast. Amber Fry had arranged for all the wives and children to stay in a separate hotel, which was great of her. When I finished breakfast and went back through to the hotel lobby, all the players were there with their wives, partners and families. I thought it was a lovely sight. All the players were wearing their new suits, the majority of them still sporting the tags, which I found amusing. Seeing how proud all their families looked, I remember thinking, I so wish for these guys that they win today. My needs and desire aside, these guys deserved it, they had been through a lot, especially the ones who had made it through the previous season. And the families, look at all these happy faces, what will this mood change to in six hours time?

Darren asked me if we were organising anything for after. I don't organise anything, because if you do, it looks like you're pre-empting which can be dangerous. Without me knowing, the club had arranged a room for after the event no matter what the outcome.

I stood outside the hotel smoking about fifty fags next to Barry who had a fucking Savannah in his mouth. Suddenly Bob came out and said, 'We have an issue.' I said, 'What is it?' 'Huddersfield have put T-shirts on every single seat in their allocation. Our end looks completely bare.' Huddersfield Town were going into the match unbeaten in the league for like twenty-nine games and had a 'Believe' campaign going on, and these T-shirts were saying exactly that.

I was proper pissed off by this. We were already playing a team with a fucking massive fan base, the fact that they were only down the road from Manchester didn't help, so we knew they were going to heavily outnumber us. Had it been Wembley it may have been different, but now we had these blue-and-white shirts against us too.

Huddersfield hadn't mentioned this arrangement to us, and I felt maybe the right thing for them to have done was give us advance warning of this. I would have like them to have come to us and said, 'Look, we are looking to do this, and we're giving you the option to do something similar.'

Barry popped up and said, 'Look, fuck them, fuck their banners, fuck their T-shirts, fuck their unbeaten run, it's about the football, it's about the two teams.' And he had a point. I was ready to let our football do the talking.

I arrived at the stadium and for some reason something didn't feel right. There were lots of speeches going on, the chairman of The Football League got my name wrong, the match sponsor was a Huddersfield fan, believe it or not. I felt very uncomfortable. I thought, 'Fuck this, I'm going for a fag,' and I went outside and that's where I was lifted, seeing all the Posh walking by in full voice, everyone coming over asking for autographs and pictures: it was amazing.

I went back in and received the team sheet, and as soon as I saw that, I knew that we would win that match. Huddersfield had set it up like it was an away match for them and for whatever reason they had left their leading goal scorer out. This is the equivalent to us leaving Mackail-Smith on the bench: they were certainly more worried about us than we were about them.

I went and sat in my seat and I ended up having The Football League Chairman and his mate sitting next to me, so instead of me having the end seat like the Huddersfield chairman would have, I'm three seats in. This really pissed me off: the biggest game of my life and I can't curse or say how I feel because I've got these two dignitaries beside me.

HUDDERSFIELD TOWN V.
POSH, LEAGUE ONE PLAY-OFF FINAL, OLD TRAFFORD

Peterborough United returned to the npower Championship at the first time of asking after a stunning 3-0 victory over Huddersfield Town at Old Trafford with all three goals coming in the final 15 minutes. Posh, wearing their brand new black Nike away kit, got the game underway at Old Trafford with over 15,000 supporters behind Paul Jones' goal backing Darren Ferguson's blue and white army. Ferguson's men were inches away from making the perfect start on six minutes as Craig Mackail-Smith raced onto a clever flick from Lee Tomlin, but his shot was deflected onto the foot of the post by a defender and out for a corner kick. A snap shot from George Boyd from 25-yards was gathered by Ian Bennett on nine minutes as Posh continued to create opportunities in front of goal. Huddersfield, backed by close to 30,000 supporters won their first corner kick on 11 minutes as Roberts' cross deflected behind via Grant Basey. They won their second as Lee Peltier's header deflected behind, but Basey defended well to prevent Peter Clarke sending his header towards goal. Goalkeeper Paul Jones produced his first save of the afternoon on 20 minutes to claim a Daniel Ward looping header after Mark Little had sliced his clearance at the near post following a long throw. Mackail-Smith was causing the Huddersfield defence all sorts of problems with his pace and work-rate and his efforts nearly yielded a first goal as Bennett and Hunt collided, but the full-back did well to get back and clear. Tomlin received a caution on the half hour mark for a foul on Peltier, somewhat controversial in the former Rushden and

Diamonds winger's opinion as he felt he got a touch to the ball as he slid in to make the challenge. Posh had a penalty appeal turned down on 32 minutes as Wesolowski took a tumble in the box, but the referee waved away the protests. Lee Peltier was then lucky to escape a red card after a crude lunge on Wesolowski, but the referee Steve Tanner quickly produced a yellow card. Posh got themselves into their own problems though, failing to clear when they had the opportunity. Jack Hunt was then carded for a foul on Tomlin before the Posh player saw a shot blocked after a slick build-up. Jones tipped a curling Roberts free-kick around the post on the stroke of half time after Boyd was penalised for a foul on Arfield. The resulting corner kick fell kindly for Arsenal loanee Benik Afobe, but his turn and volley went wide of the target. On the stroke of half-time, Posh had a glorious opportunity to open the scoring as the ball fell nicely for Mackail-Smith, but his toe-poked effort rolled inches wide of the post.

I remember going in at half time cursing Craig, who should have put us 2-0 up, and getting evil daggers off Kirstine. They were re-showing bits of the match on the TV and I remember saying to Barry, 'This is typical, us missing chances, and Huddersfield will end up making us fucking pay!'

There were no changes made at the interval by either side as the second half got underway with Posh now kicking towards their noisy contingent of supporters. Skipper McCann curled a 25-yard free-kick onto the roof of the net on 50 minutes after Boyd was upended by Peltier. Ward sliced a shot wide on 53 minutes as Huddersfield began to assert themselves on the game. The crowd were definitely playing their part in proceedings, the Posh fans may be outnumbered, but they are in great singing voice. Lee Clark's men were inches away from scoring on 58 minutes as Danny Ward cut inside from the left and fired an unstoppable left-foot shot onto the top of the crossbar. Posh were dealt a blow just after the hour mark as Basey was withdrawn with a hamstring injury, Charlie Lee coming on in his place at left-back. Lee entered the fray with Huddersfield enjoying their best spell of the game and it took a while to adjust to the pace of the game, cautioned for a very high challenge on

Kay. Town were still on top as the game entered the final 20 minutes with Roberts and Kilbane both seeing efforts blocked by a hard-working Posh defence. The Terriers were certainly living up to their name, again they were fortunate to escape with a caution when a red card could well have been shown to Kay as he chopped down Mackail-Smith as he bore down on goal. Posh got the goal they deserved on 78 minutes as Grant McCann's free-kick was glanced home at the near post by Tommy Rowe and less than two minutes later it was 2-0 as Boyd picked out Mackail-Smith and his shot took a deflection and wrong-footed Bennett in the Huddersfield goal. The crowd went mental, absolutely mental. It was Mackail-Smith's 35th goal of the campaign and 99th of his career at Posh. It got even better for Posh as in the last 10 minutes of the game, a sublime free-kick from Grant McCann was whipped over the wall and into the top corner, sending the Posh fans into delirium. Three minutes of stoppage time passed without incident and Posh were back in the Championship!

Final Score: Huddersfield Town 0-3 Posh

Huddersfield: Bennett, Hunt, Kay, Clarke, Naysmith, Kilbane, Peltier, Arfield (sub Lee 82min), Ward (sub Cadarmateri 79min), Roberts, Afobe (sub Rhodes 82min). Unused subs: Colgan, McCombe, Gudjonsson, Novak.

Posh: Jones, Little, Basey (sub Lee 63min), Zakuani, Bennett, Wesolowski, McCann, Boyd, Tomlin (sub Ball 85min), Rowe (sub Whelpdale 85min), Mackail-Smith. Unused subs: Richardson, Langmead, Mendez-Laing, Newell.

Huddersfield had a good twenty minutes worth of the possession in that second half, but even then didn't do anything really to warrant winning the match accept maybe hitting the bar once. When McCann whipped in one of the best free kicks you'll see towards the head of Tommy Rowe everyone around me was going nuts, and all I could do was look at the watch. Typical us, we never sit on our laurels, we go straight back up and score again thanks to Craig. At this point my family and Barry were going ape shit, but again I didn't react. I think at that point we had about eight minutes left.

McCann then stepped up with an unbelievable free kick and then I went nuts, so much so that I think I actually French-kissed my father-in-law, it was one of those real surreal moments in life: my children being born, marrying Natalie, great moments; losing my mother, dark moments; but this was one of those bright-light moments, and Barry was right, there was no better feeling than to get promoted through the play-offs!

I remember on about the 89th minute Barry leaning over and tugging me saying, 'Come on get down here, we're going on the fucking pitch!'

As I was descending down I noticed lots of Huddersfield fans leaving and throwing their 'Believe' T-shirts onto the pitch, which I didn't like. I thought that was a bit of sour grapes on their part.

The final whistle went and we were all able to celebrate together on the pitch in front of our 15,000 supporters. It's moments like that that you would like to capture and stick in a bottle and relive that feeling at your request. It was incredible.

I remember standing there on the pitch trying to take it all in and thinking, 'Wow, three promotions in four years!' Bringing Fergie back was now vindicated, the shit season prior had been wiped out, and I hoped massively that Posh fans had forgiven me for all the mistakes I had made.

I went through to the dressing room with the players, drinking beer, spraying champagne, did some interviews. I spoke with my dad on the phone, who had watched the game out in the States. I then went back pitchside and saw Lee Tomlin holding my trophy, so I took it off him. I had been waiting a long time to get a trophy. I had dreamed of getting a trophy, so this was my trophy.

I went back up to the box, where my family and other Posh supporters were and took the trophy, at which they all cheered. I went outside the directors' box area and saw Dean Hoyle, the Huddersfield owner, who was with his teenage son, and his son looked in a bad way. I went over and sat with the pair. I said, 'I don't know what to say, it was always going to be one of us sitting here like this. You have a great football club and a very good manager in Lee Clarke, and I'm sure you will win the league by a landslide next season.' I ended the conversation with the best bit of advice I could have given him. I said, 'Stick with what you are doing and you will do alright!' I liked Dean, he was a nice guy.

I rate Lee Clarke a lot as a manager, as well, and I think he is a lovely guy. I truly hope that Lee can bring future success to Dean and Huddersfield Town Football Club. So I will be rooting for them to succeed.

I appreciate that I am not the most popular person with Huddersfield fans due to my silly comments at out victory parade following the play-off final. Bear in mind I was caught up in the moment and had also suffered serious verbal abuse when leaving Old Trafford with the trophy whilst with my wife, from Huddersfield fans. I shouldn't of taken frustrations out by making those comments and I apologie for any offence caused.

We went back to the hotel, the trophy still in my grasp, and I was told all that was put on was a few bottles of wine. So I said, 'Fuck that, open the bar up and I will foot the bill!' I think the tab was stopped at like £7k! We basically all got pissed for about nine hours. I remember sitting out in the courtyard area of the hotel speaking with Barry, the gaffer, the families of a lot of the players, it was great. Former players like Shaun Batt and Aaron McLean came along, which showed their affinity to the club but also to the manager.

The one thing that Darren gets from his players is love, they love playing for Darren Ferguson. Each and every one of them would run through a brick wall for that man, and that speaks words. I think that's why our season was so poor before, due to the hangover. If you lose a parent, it's going to take a long time to get over that, and that back end of the season I realised just what Darren meant to these guys, especially the younger lads in the side. So for these ex-players to come and join us in the celebrations was great.

When I eventually got to bed I slept with the trophy, all the way through until the morning. We had to be up at six so that Natalie could return to the States and I would carry on back to Peterborough for the parade. The council very gracefully put this on for us, paying for a open top bus, etc.

When I arrived back at the club I actually sat and had a meeting with the gaffer to discuss Plan A. We went through with Barry the list of players we wanted in and the list of players we wanted out, because we knew after the parade everyone would be going off on their well-deserved holidays, and I was heading off the Bahamas for twenty days.

SUMMER OF HARMONY, CONFUSION AND SURPRISES

Kelvin Langmead, James Wesolowski, and Aaron Davies were all on the manager's out list, and had all been told. We knew Craig was going, that was a certainty. There were also a few surprise names in Charlie Lee and Chris Whelpdale, two players who had both been offered new contracts but both turned them down. Darren and I had made an agreement that we weren't going to just let players run down their final year with the club and if possible we would sell them.

Charlie was a folk hero for us, and Whelps had done great for the club also, but in honesty I don't think Darren saw them in his starting eleven at Championship level. Had that been different then maybe he would have fought harder to keep them, but Gillingham came in for the pair offering them big money to play in League Two and they took it, so hats off to the guys.

We were off to a beautiful resort in Portugal at the start of July so we were going to do what we had to do now, and then go our separate ways for a small break. The gaffer went off to Spain for a couple of weeks and Barry was left behind to sort out the two lists. We agreed that we were going to cut our squad down to eighteen or nineteen full timers and then complement that with two or three loan players.

The money received on going up into the championship is a minimum of £4 or £5 million extra on top of the budget, but remember at the same time everyone's wages go up also, so in reality there isn't a lot left over. But the good thing was that I didn't need to put any of my own money into it, so the club could stand on its own two feet.

Our targets going into the Championship were to compete and be respectful, unlike last time. Don't set unrealistic targets, just aim to stick points on the board and to play football the right way: none of this long ball shit that you see some teams do. We were sticking with the young and hungry policy – remember, Grant McCann, Boydy, Joe Lewis, Tommy Rowe, Gabby had now all played at Championship level.

This time round I made sure there was no pressure on anyone, especially the manager. I just wanted us to go in there with our heads held high, make London Road a fortress, a very difficult place for teams to come and get anything out of the game, and aim for 50 points.

On our list to get in was Bournemouth left-back Rhoys Wiggins, who was going to cost us £300,000. The gaffer's Number One target was centre-back Jason Pearce, who was again from Bournemouth. Bennett we knew would do fine but Gabby still hadn't signed an extension at that point and we were also conscious of his injury record.

With Jason Pearce, we agreed a deal of £500,000, but in the end he chose the wages of Portsmouth. This really annoyed me, actually, because again it shows the contradiction that goes on in football. We are a football club who likes to run a very tight ship and we live within our means, whereas Portsmouth, who went belly-up owing over £100 million and actually going into administration only twelve months later, beat us in the race for a player over wages. What's wrong with that picture?

I remember whilst out in the Bahamas I was getting phone calls every day from Barry that were frustrating the hell out of me. The gaffer met with Pearce, whom we had permission to speak to. We actually offered him a pretty good package and I think Portsmouth offered him an extra few grand a week and we just couldn't match it, we couldn't do it. Portsmouth get 17,000 people through the door every week, you know, and we get 8,000 if we're lucky.

We went after Danny Green from Dagenham but it was never a goer because he was a Charlton boy, and Charlton ended up buying him. They ended up snatching Wiggins too, by paying silly money wages-wise, I say with great bitterness.

Steve Gleeson and Sam Baldock were two names at the top of our wish list. I'd loved Sam Baldock for about two years, I saw him as a £5 million striker in a year's time. The manager scouted him and agreed with me. Gleeson was young and exciting and ticked all our boxes – remember Frecklington was on the transfer list at that point and was on the way out the door so we needed someone to fit into that diamond.

We eventually agreed a deal with Pete Winkleman to get both players for £1.6 million. Pete wanted the money up front, but we were gambling on being in the Championship so I wanted the payment to be over three years. We eventually came to a deal, only to get a phone call a day later from Pete saying that his manager Karl Robinson was unhappy with the decision and was threatening to resign. So now we could only have Baldock and not Gleeson. So that was a set back.

Baldock came to the club to meet the gaffer and straight away the manager got a bad feeling from the player. He rang me and said, 'Chairman I'm not getting a good vibe from Baldock, there's no way I'm letting you spend £1 million for the boy.' I was gutted, and you can see how well he's done since joining West Ham. He will go on to be a great striker, but if the manager doesn't want him then the manager doesn't want him.

We had agreed a deal with Dean Cox from Leyton Orient, a decent midfielder who was dangerous with set pieces. We had agreed a deal of £400,000 with Orient. Barry met with Dean and all the player spoke about was money: we offered him a great package but he wanted unrealistic wages for a player stepping up a level.

There was no way in the world that we were going to pay players that had never even kicked a ball at Championship level that sort of money. We are very incentive based: if you sign for us and play well then you will get rewarded and earn big, big money, but demanding a wage like that from the off was taking the piss.

We tried to get Michael O'Conner from Scunthorpe but the club didn't want to do business. Michael was coming to an end on his contract, and we offered Scunthorpe £250,000, which is what they paid Crew for him. So we offered them their money back but they turned it down.

We worked hard all summer trying to get Cody McDonald but it was clear that since the Craig fiasco Norwich were in no rush to do business with us. He ended up going to Coventry.

With Craig leaving I knew that fans would want to see a big signing to fill his boots, and I wanted to deliver. I wanted to spend £1 million on a striker, but for whatever reason it didn't happen. In all honesty I was going off on one again and looking to spend money we didn't have, so in fairness I'm glad it worked out the way it did.

Craig Alcock was on the list from Yeovil, a guy who could play anywhere along the back line, and we got him on board. Gabby had come to his senses and signed a new deal. Paul Taylor, who had been in the squad for a while, was looking very tasty indeed, so we knew that Tomlin and Taylor would be a dangerous pairing against any defence.

The gaffer identified Nicky Ajose from Man Utd. I wasn't sure about Nicky, this guy was going to cost us £300,000 and the only League experience he had had was playing on loan at Bury, but again I supported the manager. Out in Portugal, Ajose looked absolute quality: he was always the first at the training ground and the last to leave and looked pure class. Unfortunately for us, up until this point he hasn't worked out, but given the amount of money that has been invested in the lad I hope that soon changes.

We spoke with West Ham about a winger they had on their books as a youngster, Daniel Kearnes, and their response was, 'Yup, sign him up all day long.' So a deal was done with Dundalk for the boy.

Emile Sinclair was on the gaffer's radar. The kid has bags of pace and we paid just under £200,000 and pinched him from under the nose of Blackpool and a few other clubs. Barry is a great friend of Gary Simpson, the manager at Macclesfield, so the deal was done quickly. In fairness to Emile he was offered double his wages at Blackpool but he signed for us, he's that type of guy.

Scott Wooten and Ryan Tunnicliffe, we managed to get on loan from United: Wooten, a decent centre-half, and Tunnicliffe, a kid who is expected to go very far in the game. I think Paul Scholes likened him to Steven Gerard, so that was exciting. Ben Gordon, from Chelsea, was a left-back that we were told would suit us down to the ground. He was coming to us once he had finished with the England youth squad. And Josh Thompson was a centre-half from Celtic that we managed to get on loan. So the squad was coming together nicely.

On players going out, we were all praying that it would all work out for Gary Johnson at Northampton, because we knew that he would take a handful of transfer-listed players with him. He ended up taking Langmead and Davies. With Wesolowski, we ended the contract; he then signed a deal at Oldham. We also agreed terms for Nana to leave the club. You know, all these players Gary had once said would be worth money to the football club, we were now having to pay to get them off our books, it was very frustrating.

The QPR deal that we had agreed with Neil Warnock for Craig had fallen through over the summer. The deal was worth £3 million plus bits and pieces to the football club. I actually fell out with Barry over this because one minute he was ringing me saying the deal had changed because Neil couldn't get the money off his owners, the next he was ringing me saying the deal was off. Now if Barry tells me a deal is done, I'm expecting exactly that. This was clearly a deal that wasn't done!

We then had ear shot that Brighton were going to come in with an offer, and West Ham were also in the background. I told Barry to get Brighton, Leicester, West Ham and Birmingham all involved in a bidding war. I said, 'Call them all and explain that so and so has bid X amount, and generate a mass of interest.'

Leicester came in with a bid of £2 million, which we turned down. They then came back with another offer, which was £2.5 million plus add-ons which would have taken the offer up to £4 million. We accepted this offer. Leicester City then took ten days to contact Craig, and it pissed me off like crazy. It felt like they had had their bid accepted and now the were off to see if there was anyone better they could get in the meantime.

Danny Graham went to Swansea for over £3 million. I'm not being funny and no disrespect to Danny Graham but I felt personally Craig Mackail-Smith was more prolific than this lad, so that was my benchmark fee-wise. I kept thinking, do these clubs actually have scouts that know what they're on about? Do they actually know what Craig is capable of? I felt Craig deserved a Premiership team, the lower teams in the League would have seen Craig explode onto the scene.

Brighton came in with a terrible bid for something like £1.5 million over three years. Now I never get involved in transfer bids, but I actually responded to this offer personally, I wrote: 'Congratulations on your success last season, please tell your owners the Bloom brothers that I am very impressed with the way you play your football, I love your new stadium and I wish you all the best for the new campaign. However, I feel this deal is a bit rich for you.' I left it at that and I knew that would get back to the Brighton owners, and if their ego was anything like mine they would blow a fucking gasket and be straight on the phone demanding to buy Craig. I had no problem with Brighton making an offer for the lad as long as it wasn't taking the piss.

So Leicester was on the table for up to £4 million; Brighton's offer was taking the piss; and then suddenly West Ham came in with an outrageous offer: a four-year deal for Craig, a guaranteed £2.7 million over three years with add-ons that would amount to £5 million. I was absolutely buzzing: the club would be financially sound, I could take a bit of cash, and we would also have regular income each year. It was fucking perfect.

We paid Dagenham £100,000 so that we that we cancelled out Craig's 20% sell-on fee, Dagenham needed the money and it was a great deal for Posh. Then Barry called me to say that Craig had been to West Ham to meet big Sam but it didn't go well. I said, 'What do you mean it didn't go well?' 'Craig didn't feel wanted,' Barry replied. I said, 'Barry, I couldn't give a fuck if Craig doesn't feel wanted, it's West Ham!' 'Nah, he's not getting a good feeling, it's not gonna happen,' Barry said. 'Barry,' I said, 'Right, get him over to Leicester to meet Sven.' 'He feels Sven doesn't really want him either,' Barry replied.

At this point I was getting angry: a massive club like West Ham comes in but he doesn't want to go there; Leicester, a team that have bags of cash to spend, their manager is the former England gaffer Sven

Goran Erikson, and he doesn't want to go there either. Where the fuck does he want to go?

This is going on for about a week, I had a £5 million bid on the table and a £4 million bid on the table and now both of those were down the pan. I was having palpitations!

Myself and the family flew over to England, and the following day I was due to fly out to Portugal with the team, with Craig being left behind. I called Barry up and said, 'Look, if your job's worth anything to ya, you'll get on the phone to West Ham and get that deal resurrected, go round to Craig's, drag him and his fucking agent into a car and drive them to London.'

Don't get me wrong, I knew Craig had been a fantastic servant to this football club, but what the fuck is he doing umm-ing and ah-ing about West Ham? 'Get him to fucking West Ham!' I demanded.

I flew out to Portugal and when I arrived I got a call from Barry to say the deal was dead in the water and West Ham no longer wanted to do business, and to top it off they couldn't afford it. I said, 'Barry, what do you mean they can't afford it? Who's pulling my fucking leg here?' At this point I was thinking there was some kind of fucking conspiracy or something.

Then out of the blue Barry called again to tell me that Brighton were now at the table. They were offering £2.5 million up front with £750,000 in add-ons, so basically £3 million was the offer. I said, 'Barry, tell me something, has he always wanted to go to Brighton?' 'Yeah, he loves Gus,' Barry replied. I said, 'But he's never met Gus Poyet!' 'He met Gus two weeks ago,' Barry responded. I said, 'What do you mean he met Gus two weeks ago? 'Oh yeah, I gave him permission to speak to Gus,' Barry said. 'Why did you give him permission to speak with Gus, I haven't done a deal with Brighton!' I snapped. He said, 'Ah, I thought it would be good for him to speak with Gus.' Gus Poyet had basically hypnotised Craig into signing for Brighton, he had told him he was going to be his Number One summer signing, that he loved him, he adored him. And because this was to Craig's liking, it wouldn't have mattered if Barcelona had come in for him at that point, because his mind was set.

I would never have allowed Craig to meet Gus Poyet until I had accepted a deal from Brighton. Obviously Barry felt he was doing the right thing, but I didn't.

I was standing outside where all the players were having their dinner, and I remember thinking, What the fuck am I going to do? Leicester are gone, West Ham are gone, QPR are gone and all that remains are Brighton who want him by the end of the day. The club overdraft had me by the neck and we had budgeted to have Craig's sale money in by now, so I was backed into a corner, and I fucking hate being backed into a corner.

I called Barry and I said, 'Do the fucking deal with Brighton, but I'm not happy!' He said, 'Why are you not happy? It's a great deal.' 'We had fucking West Ham at the table, Barry, offering £5 million, and you're asking why am I not happy?' I snapped. 'But West Ham are no longer at the table,' he replied. 'No, but they fucking were,' I said, 'and that's where Craig would have gone had it not been for Gus fucking Poyet in the background!'

People reading this might think it's sour grapes, but this is why I wasn't happy over the whole sale of Craig. That move shocked a lot of people. I know when the players found out they couldn't believe it, they were stunned and couldn't understand why he didn't go to West Ham.

Truth be told, this was one moment in our relationship when I absolutely lost it with Baz, and called him all the names under the sun at one point in a phone conversation and hung the phone up on him aggressively. I felt bad about the way I had reacted, but money does that to people under pressure, and Barry, to be fair, doesn't take those things personally.

We eventually moved on from this transfer saga. At the end of the day, Craig will always be a legend at Peterborough United Football Club. On and off the field, he was a model professional for us, scoring 99 goals along the way. And no one more than me wishes him every success for the future. Keep in mind he was my favourite player, so to see him leave was devastating. I just wish a Premier League club had taken a gamble on him, because he deserves to be playing at the highest possible level.

I was sad that Craig didn't contact me after his move but hey, that's football for you. Other players, like Aaron, reached out, and actually came to games and even gave me a signed shirt with 'Thanks' written on it.

Out in Portugal for pre-season it was great getting to know the players. Watching them all train and seeing how these young men were responding to Darren was fantastic. Whilst watching training I said to Barry, 'We have got a new midfielder.' Lee Frecklington was incredible, he was a whole new player. Lee had been on the transfer list and was near enough out the door, but he had spoken with the gaffer before we left asking for a chance to prove himself. He admitted he was in a bad place last year and wanted to make amends. The gaffer agreed to give him a shot and thank fuck he did, Frecklington's change in form saved us splashing out £400,000 on another midfielder. We knew from last time in the Championship that Lee was very capable of playing at that level, we even turned down a £750,000 bid from Swansea for him, so Lee's commitment and hard work has paid off massively, giving the football club a £1 million asset if he continues playing the way he has been.

The sessions that the manager put on out there were incredible and the boys looked top drawer, they really did. Technically and mentally every single player looked ready. Everyone had a smile on their face. I know that some of the backroom staff wanted me to go out and spend £12,000 on wages to bring in some experience but the one person that wasn't worried was the gaffer, who was happy with what we had.

We sat and spoke in depth about how this wasn't going to turn out like the last time we were at this level, and the one thing I said to everyone was, 'Look, we may not have the biggest budget in the League, nor the biggest gates in the League but we do have the biggest heart, and that, along with respect and hard work, will keep us in this League this time round.'

The ambition was to get 50 points for the season, that was the only target. The next chapter was now upon us.

BARRY FRY

Before I bought Posh, what did I know about Barry Fry? A cheeky chappy, everyone knows who Barry Fry is. He's a guy who always has his thumbs up, a loud mouth in football, very popular.

If you ever go to a game at Wembley with him, and I have, you will see how popular he is amongst independent fans. They fucking love him. We were out having lunch in a hotel in London and everyone kept coming over asking for a picture or his autograph, 'It's Barry Fry, it's Barry Fry!' I've known Barry now for six years, and I wouldn't say it's a father/son relationship but it's a strong one.

When I first took over at Posh it was clear to see there were issues between the fans and Barry Fry. One of the first things I did was arrange a meeting with the local press, the *Evening Telegraph*, and I met up with the paper's sports editor, Alan Swann. I knew that it was important to get Swanny on my side from the off: the local press are your life blood, they can either like you, or they can fucking kill you. I met with Alan for a one-to-one in the boardroom, and one of the first questions he asked me was whether Barry would keep his job. My immediate response was, 'Barry Fry has a job for as long as he needs it.' The following day the headline of that paper was 'FRY JOB FOR LIFE' so straight away Swanny was trying to hang me with the fans from the off. (I say that in jest.)

Bob Symns, the Chief Exec at the club, told me all about the fans' dislike for Barry: he told me how Barry had been abused on the Tube in front of his wife on the way to a game, how he had been spat at, how

Mulling things over with the gaffer (Darren Ferguson) and DOF Barry Fry

Meeting Mike Tyson at London Road as we celebrated our 50th year in the Football League.

Meeting the fans in the London Road terrace

Signing Boydy from Stevenage broke the non-league transfer record

Sir Alex Ferguson at London Road

Taking over the posh – me and Barry Fry

Speaking with the gaffer at a pre-season friendly against Notts County

There's a new man in town!

Thumbs up to the Posh fans

The team celebrating promotion at Hereford
League One. Here we come!

With my wife, Natalie, and son, Calum, at London Road

With the club big guns – Barry Fry, me, Bob Symns and Alf Hand

The best way to go up. Play-off final at Old Trafford

Me and Baz with The League One play-off trophy

Me and my beautiful wife Natalie with the League One play-off final trophy in Manchester

Celebrating at Old Trafford after beating Huddersfield in the play-off final

The Holy Trinity

fans were pouring poison on his name in public which had affected his children, the gates had dropped at the club as apparent by fans felt that as long as Barry Fry was at that club they could no longer come to London Road. Protests at the ground, banners saying FRY OUT, his wife had even got used to wearing headphones to matches in order to block the abuse out. It was disgusting.

Remember I'm not stupid, I did a lot of due diligence when I took over the club. I spent over £100,000 in doing so and this allowed me to see everything, the money that was owed to him, the money he took, the money he didn't take, and I was able to see all the deals that he was involved in. All I can say is that he did his utmost best for Peterborough United Football Club, he certainly never robbed it. He had put his life on the line and even remortgaged his mother-in-law's house in order to stop the club from going into administration. The only money that Barry took from that club was in the form of a salary, which everyone who owns a football club is entitled to do, and I can tell you now that it wasn't anywhere near the amounts some people have been throwing round. That was Barry's work, and every single person who goes to work is entitled to take a salary, so why should that be different for Barry? I have proof of all of this and I only wish could make people see differently, but I know that there are some people out there that won't give a toss about the truth. They see him how they like and that's that, which is very sad indeed.

Look, I know Barry doesn't do himself any favours, he's like me in the respect that he has a big mouth, and he can get carried away. I know he has told fans to fuck off and not come to games, but when a person is pushed to breaking point, what do you think is going to happen? They're going to snap. Now I'm not saying what he said was right or wrong, but Barry has verbal diarrhoea and things he says should at times be taken with a pinch of salt. This is where at times we are kindred spirits – both with mouths that run away with themselves and a habit of getting ourselves in the headlines for all the wrong reasons.

When I came in, the club had three different supporter groups: PISA, the supporters' club (Forever Posh), and then there was the Trust. PISA was in fact set up to get Barry out of the football club. One of the first things I did was arrange a meeting with all three, because in my mind there was no point in having splinter groups, they were only going to work negatively for the club. So I worked my political charm and got the three together in a room and said, 'Listen, Barry Fry no longer owns the football club, I do. Barry is now simply an employee of mine, and if you don't support my judgment or the decisions I make then don't support me and don't support my football club. If you want to be involved in this exciting journey then I will help as much as I can. I will arrange fans' forums with you and I will do everything possible to assist you.' I basically set a stance that, 'This ends now!' I was starting a new positive vibe here and I didn't want anymore negativity surrounding us. I understood that they all wanted to stay independent, and I was honest with the Trust. They were set up so that if the club ever went tits up they could step in and take over. I said, 'Forget about me ever giving you shares in the club or having someone on the Board of Directors, because it's never going to happen.' I understand that some clubs run like that, I know that Exeter and Wimbledon, for example, are run by their trusts and they are run very successfully, but for every success story there is a failure, and I don't run my life like that, I'm afraid.

I met with the guys from PISA: Adi Mowels was the main man, a nice enough fella who is Posh through and through. I know they have their faults but I didn't have a problem with any of them. I knew how influential they were to a small group of fans, and I said from the beginning that I would assist with fans' forums, etc., and I have stuck to that promise. I told them that they had to get over their hangover on Barry Fry and move on. These guys let it engulf their life, which to me is beyond ridiculous, but there you go.

I spoke with Barry and told him to put his feelings aside for these certain individuals, that he was my employee now and I expected him to rise above it, which in fairness Barry did impeccably.

From those discussions I think I calmed everything down. I know that whenever something goes out in the press, or if something happens that the fans don't agree with, they are all straight on the bandwagon to blame Barry, but to get away from protests and anti-Barry banners is a great step in the right direction.

People don't realise that Barry is quick to jump in to protect me. When things come out that people don't like, he is there in the forefront. Barry is Director of Football and the best in the business. If Barry walked out of Posh tomorrow, I know for a fact he would get a job the same day with any other Football League side. I know that because we have had so many clubs asking for his services. He has had so many opportunities to leave, but the guy is Posh through and through and to have someone in your club that's like that is so important. If it weren't for Barry you would never have had Darren Ferguson, Craig Mackail-Smith, Aaron McLean, George Boyd, etc., etc., and you would never have had me.

I know Barry has his bad sides, who doesn't? But his good points outweigh his bad by a long shot. I don't have the time to be able to do his job, and I would never add his responsibilities to a manager, because they would then demand the king's ransom for every player. Barry sits in between the manager and myself, he listens to what the manager wants and then tries to meet those demands by doing what's best for me and the football club. He is the guy that stops me paying £4,000 a week and makes me pay £2,000. Barry could open his book and call any of the ninety-two football clubs in England and do business with them because they all know him so well.

Barry Fry got Grays off our back with £20,000 in the Aaron deal. Had he not done that, then we would have had to pay Grays £300,000. I've told Barry to sort deals out for £1,000 per week and he comes back to me telling me he has got them on just £500. He will always do what's best for Posh to the best of his ability.

Barry will always back my corner, sometimes too much, but then he will also tell me when I'm wrong, and that's important. Remember Barry has been around the block about thirty times, he's been there and done it, his contacts are second to none and he knows near enough everything you need to know in the sport, which for a club like Posh is priceless. Who else could get George Best to play for Dunstable and Barnet?

He is always telling me to stop putting so much money into the club, and to start taking some back for myself. Yes, he sacks managers for me, but that's his job. People say why don't you do that yourself? I don't do it because that's why I employ a Director of Football. His remit is the football department of the club, and that includes the first team managers: they report to him, and he reports to me.

People make mistakes, we are all human after all, but people forget Barry isn't a business man, he's a football man: a football man passionate about a football club.

All of the above justifies my reasons for keeping Barry Fry at Peterborough United. I also kept Bob Symns as Chief Exec, which is strange because usually you would bring someone in with you that you knew and trusted to take that role, but I'm not that sort of person that just bursts in and starts shaking everything about behind the scenes. The football side was different, but the backroom staff deserved their chance. Bob had worked for the club for a few years before my arrival on a pittance, and he deserved a shot. I've never once thought that maybe it's time for Barry to retire, never. We've had a few ruckuses and rows, but never have I thought of pulling the plug. The worst it ever got between us was over the sale of Craig Mackail-Smith, but that was natural enough. It was too close to home, and of course Barry was going to do and say things that he wouldn't for any other player. His daughter had been with Craig a long time and he was getting stick from all corners of his life. So I completely understand that he was in a very difficult situation, and we have since moved on from this. But that was the biggest argument we've had.

Barry has always said to me, 'Look, the day you want me to go, Chairman, we'll sit down, go through it, and I'll be off.' Keep in mind Barry is always under a hell of a lot of pressure from me, but he would never threaten to quit, and I respect that. I imagine that when Posh make the dizzy heights of the Premier League he will see that as his time to retire. If he gets a full season in the Premier League as Director of Football then he would have achieved all that he could in the game. For a guy that's in his sixties, he's fighting fit, he has bundles of energy and positivity in abundance. He is always there to pick me up, and very rarely do I need to pick him up, and that's the greatest compliment I could pay him.

At the end of the day I class Barry as a very dear friend, he is almost like family to me, and without Barry I expect I would have been rodgered left, right and centre. If he left tomorrow I'd be fucked, because I would have to come over to England for months and do his job, which is a workload I can't afford to take on at the moment. I would then have to hire a new Director of Football, but that would be a nightmare because he would be forming a strong relationship with the gaffer and barely see me, so his loyalty would then lie with the manager. Suddenly I would have no one between me and the gaffer and I'd be fucked. So Barry Fry is incredibly important to Peterborough United, and incredibly important to Darragh MacAnthony.

REFLECTION

I always said from the start that I had this madcap dream of getting to the Premier League within seven years. We are now five years in and we have had three promotions and one relegation. We find ourselves in the Championship, holding our own and playing good football, so anything is possible.

We have two-and-a-half years to get to the promised land, and OK, that's me being a dreamer, but anything is possible. If I'm honest I would be happy for us to become an established Championship football club, to get gates of between 12 to 14,000 per home game, to own our own stadium and to have a youth policy that produces kids every week. That's the dream, and we are capable of making that dream a reality.

A massive disappointment for me has been the attendances at matches. London Road has seen the most entertaining football in the country, and has seen more goals than any other football ground. What more do football fans want? The football stadium has been a huge disappointment for me, my debt to the club not being reduced disappoints me. These are all things that need working on, and that's why I work so hard to get this club to the shape I feel it should be in.

Two years ago I had a call from a guy in Asia asking if I would be interested in selling. Now my dad goes on continuously saying sell the Posh, sell the Posh, but it's not got to that stage and I hope it never does. Could I have purchased a football club that owns its own ground, has big gates, is less hassle? Absolutely. Do I regret choosing Posh? Never. I have fallen in love with this football club, so much so that my wife calls it the mistress in my life. The famous saying is that you don't choose who you fall in love with, and that is the case in this situation.

Of course if there came a time where the fans no longer wanted me, then I would step aside for the good of the club, but I have a big list that I still need to complete and I'm very driven to fulfill that list. I'm thirty-six years of age, so I have plenty of time to achieve that in. It would be great that by the time I'm fifty, my son comes on board as a director, at which stage the club will owes me nothing, we will have a 20,000-seater stadium that we own, and massive gates to boot. That would be the ultimate thing.

I want people to look at Posh like they do an Ipswich, a Norwich or a Reading, rather than being a little club out of its depth, and I will work until my fingers bleed to make that happen.

Owning a football club has been exhilarating at times, very trying, but overall it has been an enjoyable experience. It hasn't changed me as a person in any shape or form but I have certainly learnt a lot from the period. I came into it from the off on my terms, I took the way I was in business and brought it into football and that for me was important. The media issue has been a big thing during my time as owner and the fact that I have stuck my head above the sand. The business that I once owned has since long gone, yet I am still being hit all the time and from all angles, which is upsetting. If I didn't own Peterborough United Football Club they wouldn't give a toss, so overall I would say that is the only shit side to it. Now that I've owned a football club though, I would never be able to go back to not owning one. If I sold Posh tomorrow, I would go and find another club to buy. It's now well and truly in my blood.

When you're a fan you fail to see what goes on behind the scenes and fail to realise the depth of football as a whole – for instance agents. I knew agents were in the game but not to the extent that they actually are. I actually thought players had a lot of their own input into things, whereas the reality is that agents are massively influential. I've learnt how tricky the game can be from top to bottom. I've been surprised by how little power owners and chairman actually get. We are all signed up to rules and regulations from the FA, FIFA, The Football League, etc.,

etc. There is very little we as owners can actually do, which is frustrating as hell in all honesty, but again, it's a learning curve, and I am learning all the time.

People have often asked me if I have ever thought of going into football management. After reading this book I'm sure a lot of you would agree that I have a pretty good eye for a player, but in honesty I don't have the time nor the patience. Of course I have dabbled with a bit of Football Manager on the old PC in the past, and a very successful manager I was too. But of course everyone wants to be an armchair manager, we all do, but I've seen first-hand what these guys have to go through, the stress, the heartache, the frustrations, the regret. Do I need that? I think I will leave that to the professionals.

Having the managers that I have had since being owner, and the experiences I have been through during those periods allows me to appreciate Darren Ferguson. In fact my biggest worry is what I would do if Darren were to move on, because right now I couldn't tell you who I would want to manage Peterborough United other than Fergie himself. Five years into my ownership I sit here and think of everything, the highs, the lows. For me my greatest achievement in this time would be bringing Darren Ferguson back, the comeback. The previous year saw Mark Cooper, Jim Gannon and Gary Johnson all try to fill his boots but none of them, for one reason or another, worked out. After Gary we were at a crossroads and what better way to unite Peterborough United than to reunite the club with Darren Ferguson.

It was a huge gamble bringing Fergie back to London Road. Of course if it worked, happy days, but if it didn't, then I was fucked. I would have certainly lost the respect of the fans, and if you lose your fans you lose your club. I didn't want to lose my club, so bringing Darren back was probably the most inspiring thing I have done, and the greatest thing I have done whilst owning the club. Darren's return sent us to Old Trafford and gave me memories that will live in me forever, moments that I wouldn't swap for anything.

As I mentioned before, Darren's return brought a calmness back for myself. I no longer sit there worrying about this and worrying about that, I'm more able to get on with things outside football. I even wen record to say that if I fired the gaffer for a second time then I would leave the football club myself, and I stand by that statement. The only way Darren Ferguson is leaving us is to go on to bigger and better things to further his career, and with that I will stand aside and not get in his way. In fact a couple of championship clubs approached us recently about Darren. He came to me straight away and said he wasn't interested. I suggested he spoke with them, which he declined. I pray that we have at least a few more years of achieving together before Darren moves on to be a top Premiership manager, because that's where the guy is destined to be.

Darren and myself are not the only reasons Peterborough United have had success. A football club cannot be a football club without the front of house staff and the guys that work behind the scenes. We have a small family-like team who work extremely hard day-in-day-out to make sure things happen and work properly. And I appreciate all that those guys have done over the years – the media boys, the guys in commercial, the shop staff, the office girls, the ticket office staff, everyone has played a huge part in the club's success.

These next coming years for myself personally will be exciting, as my kids come of age and start coming to games. This will be a period that I'm sure will bring a tear to my eye. To see them get involved in the club will be a dream come true for me. I hope that I have left my own imprint on the game and a legacy that will last for many years at Peterborough United. I know that I am a Marmite sort of character, you either love me or you hate me. A lot of fans may look at me and think, 'What an arrogant fuck head!' but I'd like those people to understand that at the end of the day I'm just a fan – a fan who is lucky enough to own a football club. I appreciate all that I have and feel extremely blessed to lead the life I do, but I have worked extremely hard to get to where I am and I am proud of all that I have achieved.

When I took over this club, Lincoln City were a bigger club than us, Plymouth Argyle were in the Championship, Luton Town were in the Championship: that's how far we've come. The best advice that I could give to anyone is, if you love football and you can afford to do it, buy a football club. People may be against the idea, some will tell you it's a waste of money, but if you can afford it, do it. For there is no better adrenalin in the world than owning one. Don't go into it without a plan though, the plans that you map out from the start will make you or break you, but do it the right way and you will have the ride of your life.

I have only one regret since taking over the football club, one single regret. I regret not swallowing my pride that weekend and not picking up the phone to ring Darren Ferguson.

I have always said that when my time is over here I will pass the reigns onto my son Calum. I truly wish that the club stays in my family for generations. I hope one day he reads this book to see that his old man wasn't so bad, and all in all helped the club find arguably the most exciting and fruitful years of the football club's seventy-six-year history.

EPILOGUE: CHAMPIONSHIP FOOTBALL AGAIN

I have held off finishing this book, which I started writing back in November 2011, due to the fact that I really wanted to be able to add a last chapter with a so-called happy ending. This was only possible recently, on the night we lost to Southampton 3-1 at home.

I have spoken already about our recruitment in the summer not going as smoothly as we would have liked. I have spoken about how confident we all felt during training camp that this time around we all would take a different, low-profile approach to Championship football. So let me tell you all about how Peterborough United managed to hit their target of 50 points for the season, never be involved in a relegation battle, and above all play some fantastic football throughout the season.

If I can take you back to August 2011 and just before our season kicked off. You read the so called experts' views, and we were odds-on for relegation. You read some of our fans' views and again they were certain we were going down. The bookies weren't so bad but again had us at low odds for returning to League One. Hell, if anyone had seen our budget against the other teams in this league, they would have shortened those odds in an instant. Our experience, and mine personally, the two years previously, when we made a mess of competing in the Championship, with the constant non-stop drama off the field, was certainly a sobering experience, and one I was not in a hurry to repeat.

I spent most of the summer filling the gaffer's head with positive stats and encouraging him to stick to his principals on playing football, whilst at same time reminding him it wouldn't be a complete disaster if the season didn't go the way we wanted it to. I kept drumming home the need to achieve 50 points as a target for our club over forty-six games, not as a 'stay safe' target (45 is usually enough for that) but as an overall target for where we wanted to end up.

I am a stats freak so I would constantly talk about the need to win 50% of our home games, which would enable us to take approximately 35 points at London Road. I would talk about aiming for 1.1 points on average per match, trying to accumulate around 6 points on average per batch of five league games. Let's try and win 35% of every ten games, and so on.

We spoke about periods where we would take hammerings, periods where we could lose five or even six games on the bounce, periods where the knives would be out. Basically covering every kind of eventuality out there, so none of it would be a surprise or a shock if it happened. It was a weird way of going about things, but one I felt would lead us to 50 points.

The truth is that statistics-wise, half way through the season we were on course to amass around 62 points comfortably, but as had been discussed pre-season, the Championship doesn't work that way and our form in 2012 didn't mirror our form from August to end of December 2011.

A good start was essential, and playing at home first game of the season gives you a proper fighting chance, so beating Palace first game allowed us all to breathe and believe in the task ahead. Obviously destroying Ipswich live on TV 7-1 suddenly let everybody know in the football community that this so called 'little club' with the lowest attendances, the lowest budget and the youngest playing squad meant business and could actually play a bit of football as well.

Going into the Christmas period with some tough games our stats from Prozone were incredibly encouraging, showing we were in the top five sides for passes per game, possession per game, shots per game, football on the ground per game, and showing how fit the fourteen or fifteen players who played most of our games were. Losing two key components of the 'diamond formation' in Freck and McCann didn't hurt us over Christmas itself as we took 8 points from four tough games over a short period of time. But those injuries and niggles really exposed our squad going into 2012. Key players like Tomlin and Boydy lost a small bit of form and our defensive rock Gabby was never 100% fit, but he always played, which was a testament to the man's character and a hell of an example to all players in football.

Without making excuses, I would say 35% of our first eleven in most of the 2012 League games were at around 70% capacity, and playing in a period where games come thick and fast. We, as a club, will learn from this for sure, and I'd like to say this wonderful season back in the Championship has been a real education about how to cope and compete at this level. There is no doubt in mine or the gaffer's mind that we did make errors in some of our recruitment policies this season, particularly in the loan market where we probably blew over £500k on four or five players who didn't come off for whatever reason. If we had used those funds on three players who were signed full-time to our club, then maybe our second half of the season would have been a lot better.

Don't get me wrong, we recruited well in the 2012 window by bringing in Tyrone B and Shaun B for over £1.4 million, and they were excellent additions to our club and for next season onwards. But I think we missed a beat by not signing one or even two proper hard-biting defensive midfielders with energy, a tackle, and who could pass the ball. Those couple of additions would have allowed the gaffer not to rush back injured players, maybe play a little differently away from home with two of them sitting in front of the back four giving that bit of protection we sometimes lack.

Selling Ryan Bennett didn't help, as the timing of it messed us up in a big way, but sometimes those decisions are taken out of your hands. A lot of clubs were looking at Ryan, some big ones to be fair, due to him being such a good passing centre-back and also the fact he was now recognised by England Under 21s. Both Swansea and Norwich fought hard to sign him. The lad was well aware of the money on offer and asked if he could go, due to the way it would affect his family and his life. Plus I had always stated if Premier League clubs come knocking for our players and the deal was right, then I couldn't stand in their way.

The Ryan Bennett transfer was a perfect example of my policy being the correct one for a club like Peterborough United. You invest a substantial amount of money on a lower-League teenager with bags of potential; he comes in and plays a hundred-plus games for your club; helps the club to success; then he gets sold for many millions of pounds plus add-ons. That kind of business will only ever help our club improve, succeed and compete at a high level every season.

People of course complained, and called us a selling club, which I will forever disagree with. I have sold three key players in five years for millions of pounds, but only after they contributed to our club's rise through the leagues and played hundreds of games for us. Every club in the world sells a key player, as shown by Man United selling Ronaldo and Arsenal selling Fabregas or Liverpool selling Torres. That's the way it works, and we are no different, but at the same time I have turned down way more bids for players then I have accepted and in fairness always back my manager.

I think in my five years as chairman of Posh, we have spent nearly £6 million on transfer fees and bring in on average nine of ten players every season. Not to mention having recently paid out over £1 million for a striker, which not many clubs in the Championship have done this season. We may not pay the biggest wages in the business, but we are not frightened of paying a big fee for the right player.

March was really the month when we nailed down our spot for the 2012/13 Championship season. We played eight games in twenty-eight days and had three massive wins, against Blackpool, Reading and Leicester, at London Road. I could finally put away the Plan B document and start focusing on what was needed to ensure a stronger squad was in place for next season. Sure we had to wait till that evening when Southampton came to London Road and beat us comfortably 3-1, but knowing what Millwall had done at Coventry brought a huge smile to all our faces.

Eighteenth place and 50 points in one of the toughest leagues in Europe after a long twelve months certainly felt like a massive achievement for Peterborough United Football Club, and gives us a platform to kick on next year and aim above this.

Myself and the gaffer do not want to sit still and just fall over the line every year: we want to build this club from youth upwards by sticking to our policy of recruitment and go from strength to strength every season.

Let me mention Twitter briefly, as it's been an incredible social medium for me to reach out to Posh fans and other football fans. I joined last summer 2011 and have over 7,000 followers already on a locked account, which is good going. I did it because it allows me to give fans an insight into my own thoughts and feelings about matches, the club and other things in life. I have enjoyed the experience of using DMAC102 on Twitter and hope the fans have as well. The only downside is it has got me in hot water with the FA and I have already been fined this season for airing my own views and opinions.

Of course I notice that this kind of action hasn't been taken against other chairmen and directors in the Premier League, even though they have been more blatant then me with their comments, but then again this is nothing new to me in life. I keep getting told freedom of speech protects those on the web, allowing many trolls to say what they want and hurt and be abusive to others. Obviously in my case freedom of speech doesn't count and the fines will keep coming if I say anything slightly controversial, so watch this space.

Another big plus for me this season and for the future of our club was the progress made by our youth players through the hard work of Dave Robertson and Gavin Strachan. There are six players who the gaffer felt comfortable giving long-term professional contracts to: Kgosi, who is, according to Barry, going to be the best left-back that's ever come through our club youth system; Sagey, who is a sixteen-year-old giant left-sided centre-half; seventeen-year-old Peter Grant, who is a quality young centre-back, already being called up by Scotland Under 20s; Charlie Coulson, a sixteen-year-old classy midfielder whom the Gaffer thinks will go all the way; and young Jenaii, a pacy sixteen-year-old forward who excited everybody at the club, not to mention Arsenal, Chelsea and Man City who are forever in contact about wanting to see more of this lad. And finally this year has seen the proper breakthrough of Joe Newell, who has bags of skill, flair and potential, and one who the gaffer feels is ready to step into Boydy's shoes in the not-too-distant future.

Writing the above gets me more excited than all the promotions in the last few years, because I can see the landscape changing in modern football financially and within three or four years no longer will, say, 80% of clubs in the Championship have wage bills exceeding £12 million pounds per annum. This means that clubs who are ahead of the game and so-called 'punching above their weight' will have a more equal opportunity to finally have a go at promotion to the Premier League. Sure, there will still be three or four clubs with parachute payments that will still be favourites, and rightly so, to go straight back up. But as has showed with Reading, Middlesbrough and others, those parachute payments don't always guarantee an instant return to the promised land.

My own personal opinion is that all Football League clubs should not only adhere to financial fair play but should also have a minimum of five home-grown youngsters from their youth set ups in their first eleven every game. This would be good for the game, the various football communities and of course eventually the national side. A club like mine with average crowds of under 9,000 needs to either rely on a sugar daddy, a fantastic scouting network and recruitment policy, or ensure their youth has proper investment and are breaking into the first team squad.

Crewe are a prime example of a club who has no such sugar daddy, don't really spend money in the transfer market but do have majority of first teamers who are home grown. Southampton are to be envied as they have it all: a sugar daddy family of sorts who own the club; 32,000 through the gates every week, meaning they can invest £4 or £5 million on transfers; yet at same time a youth department that has produced over £50 million in players' fees through selling Bale, Walcott, Chamberlain and Co. over the last four or five seasons plus allowing their current successful side to have four or five youth-based players in their first team. That's almost the perfect balance, and to be admired, as they have finally returned to the top tier in a terrific healthy state on and off the field.

Anyhow, back to this season in the Championship. It has been enjoyable but at times exhausting for me personally as we push against many ex-Premier League clubs to establish ourselves in this terrific League. Facts show that next year will be my sixth full year as a chairman of a football club, and three of those years will have been as a Championship chairman. This gives me a tremendous sense of pride and fulfillment with this wonderful previous hobby that has now gone full circle and become a full-time obsession.

For the last twelve months I have lived, breathed and kicked every ball as Chairman of Posh. I take the defeats badly, and try and enjoy the victories, whilst at the same time worrying about the next fixture. We, as a club, have achieved many of our pre-season aims. At the same time, we have not overspent or put ourselves in any financial jeopardy whilst we have added more assets to our squad and invested well in our training ground site and our youth department.

There has been very little drama off the field this season, no ruckuses or rows with the gaffer, no doubting moments, no promotion, play-off or relegation drama – just a solid season of growth, education, consolidation and progress. What's the long-term goal, I hear you ask, for a club like Peterborough United Football Club? Below is a list of targets I have on me at all times for you to look at. Of course the cynics out there will go, 'No chance!' 'Fat chance!' and 'What a dreamer!' Then again, without cynics, we would have nothing to prove to anybody, so I hope my football club keeps proving the doubters wrong.

My Wish List and Objectives for Peterborough United Club

- Wipe out all external debt, which is mainly owed to me

- Be a competitive Championship football club

- Have one of the best training academies in the Football League

- By 2016 have five or six home grown youth talent in the first eleven

- Within the next three years have an average attendance of 12,000+

- Play in a 17,500 all-seater modernised stadium

- Own our own stadium and training facilities

- See a Peterborough United player compete at a World Cup

- Do the impossible and achieve promotion to the promised land

Please bear in mind that many of these objectives were first scribbled down by me over five years ago, when I took the plunge and decided to come up with a new hobby. A hobby that would see me buy a football club on the brink of financial ruin, based in the bottom half of League Two with an average attendance of 3,000 and one that has in fact turned into an obsession!

DMAC

THE STORY FROM THEIR SIDE

DARREN FERGUSON

The first time I met the chairman my initial thought was, 'Jeez, this guy is young!' I knew his age, obviously, but meeting him for that first time it hit home. Given his age, the two of us connected quite quickly, which was important. I think we had a lot more in common than, say, he and Keith did previously.

You have to remember that we were both taking a massive gamble, me in my first job and him, employing such an inexperienced manager to take the reins of his football club.

I had been offered the Wrexham job when I was twenty-eight. I was captain of the club, and this new owner came in and was looking to spend some money. Bryan Flynn, who was manager at the time, wanted to move upstairs into a director position, and I was offered the role of a player/manager, but I just felt at that age I was too young for the role. However, it kicked me into gear for getting my coaching badges completed.

A year or so later, when Dennis Smith left, I felt I would be in with a good chance of getting it. I felt ready for that next level, but it wasn't meant to be and they gave it to someone else. That hit me hard, I was bitterly disappointed that I was overlooked and I couldn't really see where to go from there. I knew I could carry on playing for a bit but it was getting a bit tedious, if I'm honest, and I felt that coaching was the direction I wanted to go towards and felt ready for.

I then got a call from Barry Fry telling me his chairman wanted a young manager and would I be interested? I didn't need to think twice, I was in my car and Peterborough bound! I was fully aware that a lot of young managers take a job, fail and then get no further, so I was taking a big gamble. People have often said to me, 'Why would you go into management after living with it all your life with your dad?' OK, he's had some pretty stressful times in his career, but he has seen a hell of a lot of highs, and I've always seen that first-hand. He was the first person I spoke to about the opportunity and he was all for it: he saw that Peterborough had an ambitious chairman and he knew that not getting the Wrexham job had pissed me off. My mum was also all for the idea, so the backing of my family was important. It was very much in my mind that Keith Alexander had done a good job at the club – he had lost his job after I think six defeats on the bounce, so I knew straight away that this chairman wanted nothing less than success. At the time we were just outside a play-off position and that obviously wasn't good enough for the chairman, but I'm a confident person, and I have full faith in my own ability. Although I was new in management, I had always been a leader on the pitch as a player and I felt I had what it took to succeed at Posh. The first season I came in, I fully believed we would make a play-off position. I remember we went on a good little run, we went to Shrewsbury and I watched the first half up in the stands alongside the chairman and we absolutely battered them. We went on to lose the game, and I feel that had we have won that, we would have kicked on, but it obviously it wasn't to be.

From that season, though, the chairman was able to see how I liked the game to be played, and he enjoyed it. When we originally met he asked me my favourite formation, which I said was 4-4-2. I don't know why I said that because in honesty that's my least favourite set up. I was playing three at the back at the time and it was working for us, we were playing attractive football and you ask any manager in the game they will tell you that is a massive plus to any football match.

The only pressure I was under, to be fair to the chairman, was the pressure I put on myself when I first came in – and of course carrying the 'Ferguson' name tag. But I wanted to get the lads playing decent football, and I had to work hard in getting that belief back into the side, because they had been on a bit of a bad run.

I noticed straight away that at this level we had some good players. McLean and Boyd were two players I didn't know too much about but it was obvious that they had talent; we also had your players like Hyde and Low, Tyler and Newton, who had a great depth of experience, so I felt we had a good squad. But there were obviously a few that had to go at the end of that season. When I came in, in the middle of January, the chairman had already spent a massive wedge: Hyde and Low, for instance, cost a lot of money, especially in terms of wages for League Two. Remember before I joined as manager I was still playing at Wrexham, who were in the same League as Peterborough. I remember thinking back then, with this new guy taking over and bidding a million quid on McLeod, that The Posh were not going to be in League Two for very long.

At my first meeting with the chairman I told him that I was quite happy to go with the squad we had. I told him that that first season I wanted to get a good look at the players we had, as opposed to wasting his money. I'd rather get a good in-depth look at the squad, asses it and then act on it in the summer, which is exactly what we did. We did some good business that summer. Mackail-Smith came through the door, and partnerships were forming within the group. which was a massive positive. The fact that we didn't go up the previous season grated on me a little bit, because I felt we had the squad capable of doing it. I knew that the coming season had to see success and the chairman made that absolutely apparent.

We sat down in Spain and discussed the new campaign. I told the chairman I wanted one or two players that had done it at that level, so we bought in Westwood and Keates, who were massive signings for us. We mixed that with bringing in a few young ones. The chairman was spending a lot of money and his one request to me was that he wanted a trophy, he wanted to win the League. That was the benchmark, and I was happy with how that was set.

We started the season slowly, beating Rochdale 3-0 and playing well. This kicked us on to beat Southampton in the Cup 2-1, which was a game live on the TV and our opposition were a Premiership team at that point. We then went to Rotherham and got battered, which put our feet back on the ground. This was followed with a loss against Chesterfield and then we drew at Morecambe, so we didn't have the best of starts.

After the Morecambe match the chairman, who was down at the time, told me that he wanted to see me and my staff in my office. He came in and the first words he said was, 'This isn't fucking good enough!' He said, 'I ain't gonna sack you, but I'm just letting you know that drawing to fucking Morecambe ain't good enough.' It wasn't a wake-up call because I already knew the situation and what we had to achieve from the season. I think the following game we went to Accrington and we beat them 2-0 and I believe that led to a little run.

The chairman's words of wisdom to me at that stage were him making me aware that poor results weren't good enough, and he wasn't going to stand for it. He had made his point very, very clear; it was clear as day. I had a meeting with my staff and I said, 'Look, we're only going to get one bite of the cherry here, we've gotta get better results.' It wasn't for the want of trying, but we needed to get a good run together and quickly. As I said, from that point onwards we found some form, went on a good run and I think when it came to Christmas we were finding our range. It was against us and MK Dons, really, who unfortunately pipped us to it.

The conversation we had with the chairman in the office that day had obviously done its job to a degree. His dedication to the football club is second to none and I think that shows to everyone, but for me coming into management it was a big eye opener to see how hands on he actually is. I'm not saying that's a bad thing, but I wasn't expecting it, and at times it was hard to deal with. The chairman's best form of contact is email, he loves it, and for me just retired from playing I wasn't all that clued up on emails. I preferred communication over the phone or face to face. Obviously, with the chairman living abroad, email is his preferred type of communication, and these emails are like war and peace.

The chairman is a big stats man, he loves them, and I will get emails after matches on all the stats from the game and where he felt we went wrong, and the rest, and these are regular. Back then I would be like,

'Fucking hell, another email! I can't be arsed to speak to him for a few days.' As time went on I think I learnt to grow with this issue and it's like second nature now, of course.

Don't get me wrong, we speak on the phone a lot, more so now than before, but that was more my doing than his. He loves being involved: not in the sense that he's in the dressing room, like a lot of chairman are, but that he wants to know what's going on and he wants to be appreciated. To which he has every right: the man's put about £10 million into the football club, and I'm mega-appreciative of him and he knows that. But it was certainly something I had to get to grips with at the start. Remember if we lose a football match, then no one is more pissed off than me, and it comes fast and furious. I speak with the team. then I need to speak to the press. and then I get an email... It's like, 'Fucking hell!' Now, he will rant and rave a bit on the phone, and then call me back half an hour later to say, 'Well, maybe I was a bit harsh there.' He's a winner, at the end of the day, and I fully accept that, and in honesty he is only trying to get his feelings out which he is fully entitled to do.

I can remember once when we had a proper full on barny, a face-to-face jobbie. It was back when we were in League One the first time around and we were playing Yeovil at London Road. I remember it really well because it was the day of my wife's best friend's birthday and I was fucking cursing him the whole way up north.

Joe Lewis had a bad game, like a real bad game, and we were beaten 3-1. When we got back into the dressing room after the game I could see in Joe's eyes that he had gone. Some of the lads were having a go, and I called for it to stop. It certainly wasn't the right time for me to rip into him. I came out of the dressing room and David Oldfield was outside waiting for me. He said, 'Gaffer, the chairman wants to see you and the management team in his office right away.' We went up, and inside the office were the chairman and Barry Fry. I was welcomed with the words, 'What the fuck is going on?' He continued, 'What the fuck have you done with my goalkeeper?' which I thought was a bit harsh. I said 'I've not done anything with *our* goalkeeper, he's just had a stinker!' 'Well, why's he having a stinker?' the chairman replied. It got to the point where he was talking over me and I tried to speak again, and he just said, 'Just shut the fuck up!' I stood up and said, 'Right, that's it, you can fuck off, I'm not being spoken to like one of your muppets!' I went to walk out of the office and Barry tried to stop me. I turned back to the chairman and we were face to face, and the chairman is someone I would recommend you do not go face to face with, because he's a big fucker, but I stood my ground. It was obvious that he had taken offence with what I had just said. He said, 'If you speak to me like that again, I'll put you through that fucking door!' It wasn't the best time to be having this ruckus – the boardroom, which was next door, was packed full of directors and other people, and the pair of us were not whispering our thoughts.

I left the office with my staff and went up north to this party and the chairman went back to Spain. I don't think we spoke for several days. It was very childish and I think it took Bob and Barry to pester me into ringing the chairman. That is the only time that I can remember that we have actually had a big, big bust up.

The chairman doesn't like shrinking violets, he doesn't want people bowing down to him all the time, and I'm the same in the dressing room. I have no problem with my players throwing opinions at me, as long as they have substance behind those opinions and the chairman's the same. Don't get me wrong, I don't like arguing with the guy, but I'm always going to put forward my views and I think he respects that. In the end it was a one off: we're both winners and we both hate losing. The flip side is that in my opinion, if you have a group of people that all want the same thing then I'm a big believer that you'll get it.

The guy likes to keep me on my toes and that's fine, that's his job. And in fairness he will put ideas into my head that may not have been there. He was getting anxious with Micah Hyde's form towards the end, especially given the wages he was on at the time. This turned out to be my first big decision as manager. Micah was my captain, and he was virtually the same age as myself, he did very well at League Two and I had a very honest chat with him after the promotion. I told him I wasn't sure how many games he would be involved in in League One, and I changed my captain. He wasn't happy with it, but he accepted it, and sometimes as a manager it's key to do things gradually. Me putting someone else in as captain was doing it gradually.

The thing you have to do with captains is allow them to thrive in the role. They need to be able to deal with their own responsibilities. They have a very important voice that needs listening to, and they all need full respect in the dressing room, but as soon as they start taking the piss or start thinking that they are bigger than everyone else, then that's the time to nail them. Micah had just got to the stage where he was getting left out of certain games, and I remember he turned up late for a training session and then again on a match day. I bit my lip originally but then he had Dominic Green under his wing, and he was then being late also. So the coming game, I can't remember which one it was, I left Micah out all together, and he blanked me. It wasn't the right time to deal with it at that point, but in my mind I felt that if we won the game I would deal with it after. We won the match and I nailed him in the dressing room afterwards in front of everyone.

I said, 'What sort of fucking role model do you think you are trying to be? You've been late for a game, late for training, you've got a young kid here who's learning the ropes and he's fucking being late now as well!' He tried coming back to me and I said, 'Look, you know you're speaking bollocks. If you want to fuck off just fuck off, because you're no use to me like that.' He said, 'But I don't want to leave.' I said, 'Well, if you carry on like that then that's exactly what's going to happen.' After that he was fine, but once someone takes the piss like that you can't let them get away with it because they think, 'Well hang on, it's one rule for him and another for us.' So Micah left the club.

But I don't always agree with every opinion the chairman has. Dean Keates is a good example, the chairman didn't feel Keatesy was good enough for the Championship and in truth he probably didn't play enough, we missed his experience at times. The chairman knows he has to trust me, I've got to manage it, and he does. He may say, 'Well Keates isn't good enough,' and I'll say, 'Well he is,' and then the chairman will do what he is very good at, he will say, 'OK, well I'll buy you so-and-so for X amount.' That makes things very difficult, because I might think,

Well fucking hell, I could do with him, but then I want Keatesy also... So he likes trading, and he's good at it.

The one thing you can be sure about the chairman is that he has a very good eye for a striker. Over the years, the forwards he has thrown into the mix have been more successful than mine, but I'm sure that will change of course! He put McLean and Mackail-Smith on the radar, and Tomlin. Paul Taylor he will argue about, as he was definitely my find, but this is healthy – this is what makes Peterborough United so exciting. Hatch and Rendell were mine, but look, we made money on both. The difficulty was that whilst Aaron and Craig were at the club you were never going to get anyone of any great quality in who wanted to sit on the bench all season. My one main regret in this matter was not bringing Simon Jackson in, but we live and learn.

When I arrived, we had Aaron McLean, who was a very good striker, and Mackail-Smith due to arrive. A short while after my arrival I heard news that Craig had changed his mind on the deal. I went to his home and met with him, his agent at the time, and his dad, and it was apparent the lad didn't want to play for Posh. I think ironically he felt under pressure from Barry. I knew very little about Craig Mackail-Smith but Barry and the chairman gave the lad glowing reports so I knew this was important. I told Craig exactly where I wanted to take the club, etc., and to be honest we got on very well, but he didn't want to sign. He was getting tempted by other clubs, which wasn't helping the situation, but in the end we talked him around and the rest is history as they say.

But Craig was a very important signing for us. He debuted against Wrexham and my first thoughts were, Fucking hell, he's catching pigeons, this boy! He was running everywhere, and to me confirmed why everyone was so excited about this signing. Another massive challenge I came up against during my era first time round was getting rid of my friend and goal-keeping coach, Andy Dibble. This was a very difficult situation. I'd known Andy for many years and we were good friends, but it had come to the point where I had had to give him a few warnings about certain things, and the chairman was all over me at the time about how minimal the improvement of the keepers was. The chairman was all over me with him, he said to me, 'Look, what are you doing about the situation?' and I said 'I'm aware of the situation, I've got it covered.' We had our first win of the season against Reading and then we battered Newcastle in the Cup, so things were picking up. We went to Blackpool and it was probably the most disappointed I had been, because we just didn't turn up. In the dressing room after I think Andy's mobile phone went off. I can't be completely sure but I'm pretty certain.

Now this is weird this, it's a strange story. My wife's from Preston, and after the Blackpool match I stayed down and we stayed at Trevor Hemming's hotel (the fucker that sacked me from Preston). We went for a meal and I remember saying to Nicola, 'I'm going to get rid of Dibs.' She said, 'You cant!' I said, 'I can, I've made up my mind.' 'Why?' she said. 'He just isn't doing what I want him to do and I feel I need to make a change.' My wife knows what I'm like: when I've made a decision, I stick by it. I phoned Dibs the next morning and said, 'Look, I need to meet you.' He said, 'Why, what about?' I said, 'I'll tell ya when I meet ya,' so he sort of knew, he kept texting me and I didn't reply, and calling which I just ignored. We met and I said, 'Dibs, I'm getting rid of ya.' He asked why and I explained that I had asked him to do this, told him to do that... and look, this was fucking difficult, he was pretty emotional and all the rest of it but at the end of the day, in the job that I'm in, you will come across times when you have to do and make decisions that are difficult on a personal level as well as a professional one. I still speak to Dibs, and personally I have nothing against the guy, but I had to do what was best for the football club. I stand by that decision today, it was definitely the right thing to do.

With these tough decisions come great moments, and its about taking the rough with the smooth. Hereford for instance was a great day, and for some reason that one took a long time to sink in, it was so intense. Keatesy's goal was a fantastic one and big Joe had a very good game, in fact for my money Joe Lewis was the best signing we made that year. I remember after playing Morecambe saying to the chairman, 'Look, if we buy that goalkeeper we will get promoted,' and I remember Barry ringing me one evening saying we had just signed him for half a million quid. I was like, 'Fucking hell!' At League Two level, paying £500,000 for any player is very ambitious indeed, so Joe's signing was a key part of that first promotion. The signing of Charlie Lee was another massive one for the club. Charlie was a big part of the puzzle that season and it took me a long time to get the deal done. There were about sixteen clubs in for the lad, and clinching that deal was important.

I called the chairman after that game and to me he seemed a bit down actually, he was unusually chilled. I was fucking buzzing and was expecting him to be the same. I think MK Dons had won again which made it difficult for us to win the League, and maybe that was playing on his mind, I don't know. But when he came over he seemed to be a bit happier, and we knuckled down and started again really.

That was the time when I really thought, 'Fuck, this guy doesn't stop.' We had literally just gained promotion and the chairman was like, 'Right, we need to get out of this league!' That showed the guy's drive and desire. We stuck with the nucleus of the squad, Boyd, McLean, Mackail-Smith, we added one or two to the mix but overall the side was a good one for League One level.

Once again we started the season poorly, beating Milton Keynes followed by Leeds really kick-started our season and gave us the belief that we had a good opportunity here. I remember before the MK game I received an email from the chairman saying he wasn't happy. Now one thing with these emails or these tiffs we have, they always seem to have a positive effect. That may just be coincidental, but their timings were always right, because after each one we would end up going on a run, and I suppose that's his job – he motivates the motivator and in this job that is very important indeed.

Before that match I went up to the boardroom and Barry said, 'I need to speak to ya.' He said, 'Look, I don't know what's going on but the chairman's got the hump with ya, his thinking of getting rid of ya.' I said. 'What the fuck, for what?' He then handed me a bit of paper with a list of managers on it. I said, 'Are these in fucking line to replace me?' He said, 'Yeah.' I said, 'Well that's fucking good of him ain't it... Well, he can fuck off if he's going to start playing those mind games with me.'

Now he doesn't know this, but I was so, so close to quitting before that Milton Keynes game, because I wasn't going to have any of that. I went to and fro for a fair while over the situation and couldn't believe what I had heard.

I was shell-shocked. My chairman had lined up about four different managers to replace me whilst I'm still in the job. I spoke with Rooster, spoke with my missus and I spoke with my dad. My dad said, 'Look, go to MK, beat them and then quit after the match' and that's what I intended to do. In the back of my mind I was thinking, 'Is he taking the piss and trying to give me a kick up the arse?' But if that was the case then he was taking a bit of a gamble here, and he knew that by doing this it was like showing a red rag to a bull. It would be the same as me saying to him, 'Ah, I'm not happy, here is a list of four teams I'm interested in going to.' I'd be out the door in an instant. I went up to the boardroom on my own and I phoned him, he was in Spain at the time. He picked up the phone and he said, 'Alright?' I said, 'Not fucking really!' 'Why?' he said. I said. 'You fucking tell me why I'm not alright!" I lost my rag with him, and as the conversation went on he bit back a bit. We had a lengthy chat and I think if he's honest he will admit that he maybe took it too far that day and took a massive risk. I was so close to leaving, I really was.

Look, the chairman's a successful man, and he wouldn't be in the position he's in now if he didn't motivate people and get people striving for the success that he has achieved. I don't know what his thought process is like but he must sit there and think, 'Right, how can I get him motivated, how can I get him to step it up a level?' and to be fair I need that, I really do. Don't get me wrong, he knows I'm good at my job, but as I said before he is the person who motivates the motivator and that is key. But there are ways and ways of trying to motivate someone.

At the end of our League One promotion, I went out to Rome to watch United in the European Cup final. I remember being at Flamenzi airport when I received a phone call saying, 'Would you be interested in speaking to Reading?' I phoned Barry and I said, 'Look, Reading want to speak to me.' He said, 'What do you want to do?' 'Well, it's Reading,' I said. Barry contacted the chairman and he wasn't happy in the slightest.

'Fucking Reading? Why would you wanna speak to them?' he said. Then it came out in the paper, and the chairman then put a statement out along the lines of it was like taking a bird out on a date whilst you already have a partner, etc., so making it very clear that he didn't approve.

He told me straight up that if I spoke with them then I wouldn't be coming back, so it was a bit messy. I decided that I needed to go out and see him in Spain, so I flew out and we sorted it out. I know he thought that I had put it out in the public domain but that was bullshit and it didn't come from me. I certainly wasn't going to do anything behind his back, and I needed his permission to speak with Reading. But in the end it didn't come to that. I wanted to, in the back of my mind I was thinking that maybe I had taken Posh as far as I could take them. When I went out to Spain and sat and spoke with the chairman I felt more confident that my job was not done here, so that made my mind up.

The chairman didn't have a clue about West Brom until I told him, and they were far more aggressive that Reading, believe me, and that wasn't just a one-off. I just turned them down and then told the chairman about it later on. QPR were another club that enquired about me two or three times but that was never going to happen. It was pre-season for the Championship and my staff were all sat down and signed new contracts. We all had a nice meal together, which was nice. I was buzzing, to be fair, and very excited about the season ahead. My main fault was that I believed too highly in the players: I really felt that we had a chance to do something there with that group, but the reality was that we were well off the pace, and when you start the season poorly its like a snowball effect and that's when you start to have problems.

When we sat down in the summer, he was asking, 'What we need, do we need experience, do we need this, do we need that?' but the reality was that experience costs a lot of money – money that was far greater than our wage bill, so I more or less turned the proposal down. Now I'm like everyone else, I don't like making mistakes and it's hard to admit when you have done so, but in that season I knew straight away I had made a mistake in not bringing in experience, and it took me a while to realise that and admit that mistake. I felt that our current crop would be fine and that just wasn't the case.

We went to Newcastle and myself, the chairman, Bob and Barry all had a good chat at the hotel before the game. Myself and the team began boarding the bus and the chairman came on also. This was a first, and I felt that he was doing it to see what myself and the players were up to. I didn't like the idea: I couldn't say no, but I wasn't happy with him travelling with us to the match. Barry joined him on the bus and I was sure they were doing it to see if I had lost the dressing room. It made me uncomfortable.

We lost the game 3-1 and got battered, and I received an email from the chairman which I didn't reply to because I needed to calm down and reflect. Barry phoned me the next day, whilst I was still asleep actually, and said he wanted to meet me. We met and he came out with a few things that surprised me if I'm honest. He said, 'The chairman wants to get rid of ya.' Once again I was like, 'Are you fucking serious?' I gave Barry a list of players that I felt we needed to get rid of. These were players that were merely on the fringe, not 90% of the squad and certainly not players like McLean or Mackail-Smith like it has been portrayed. He said, 'The chairman wants you to ring him.' I said, 'Ah, well he can fucking ring me.' If he suddenly wanted to get rid of me there was no way I was going to be ringing him, not a chance. I was pissed off, we had just been beaten by Newcastle, the email straight after the game was saying it's a disgrace, it's this, it's the other, and suddenly here Barry is telling me the chairman wants to get rid of me. It was a few times he mentioned it during that meeting, I must add.

I just felt, 'Why the fuck does he want to get rid of me?' I'll be honest, that made me feel really, really low, and I just thought, Ah fuck it, this is only going to go one way. So, he didn't ring me, I didn't ring him. My missus was going on at me constantly telling me to ring him, which I ignored. I came in Monday morning and got called into the office to see Barry and Bob and it was just like, 'Nah it's not gonna work, this, let's call it a day.' I said, 'Fine' and that was that.

In truth there is so much more I could tell you, but I think we'll wait until my book hits the shelves.

BARRY FRY

I had a phone call one morning saying that this guy called Darragh MacAnthony wanted to meet me to discuss buying the football club. Keep in mind that by this stage I had had like twenty-odd different people showing interest, but the majority, if not all, wanted to know about the land and the planning permissions for that land and showed no interest whatsoever in the football side, which didn't sit right with me at all.

I agreed to meet this guy but I certainly wasn't holding my breath. He sent over three of his people to meet with me and we sat around the boardroom table at the club discussing the situation. I told them from the off that the club and I were in the shit, well and truly.

Darragh, I know, was fully aware of this, as he had seen the *Big Ron* documentary on TV, and instead of making him steer clear it made him more confident that Peterborough United was that club for him.

I said to his guys, 'Look, the club owes me over a million and other directors, this, that and the other.' In honesty I don't think they really believed just how bad a state the club was actually in.

I had sold my house in Portugal for £150,000, which had originally cost me £200,000; I took a second mortgage out on my property that I've lived in for over twenty years; I took my pension out early, which was £75,000. I was lucky enough to get a testimonial here with Manchester United, which was great for the community, being able to see this huge club come and play at London Road. I put all the proceeds from that into the club, and I secured the deeds of my mother-in-law's house as security for the overdraft for the football club. It was a complete and utter nightmare and I was done, I had exhausted every single avenue in getting hold of any money.

Do you know, when CH sold me the club he went straight into town and told everyone I wouldn't last a month! And maybe he was right, I shouldn't have lasted a month. But I was responsible for my staff, a group of people that were very much like family. All these staff members needed paying, all of them had families, mortgages to pay, HP on their cars, kids to feed. There was no way I was going to have all that on my conscience. No chance.

To go back to how it all started. I had been good mates with Chris Turner for a number of years and I actually gave him a coaching job at Barnet when I was manager there. He then went on to manage Peterborough United of course, and whilst at Posh he called me one morning asking if I knew of any good centre forwards, so I gave him Ken Charlery's name, after a few months of having Kenny onboard he called me again to say that Kenny wasn't performing, I said 'Where are you playing him?' 'On the wing' he replied, I said 'Chris, Kenny is a striker, play him as a centre forward!' The rest as they say is history as far as Ken Charlery is concerned, Chris then invited me into the royal box at Wembley when Posh played Stockport County in the 1992 Play-Off final, it was their incidentally that he introduced me to a guy called CH. CH was a *big* businessman and successful at that, and I know that sometime after Chris had taken over as chairman at Posh CH was going to buy the club from him, but it didn't materialise for one reason or another.

In 1996 I got sacked from Birmingham, and on my return home that day I had about a hundred and fifty messages on my answer phone, thirty-eight of which were from Chris Turner. I got back to him the following day and it was apparent he wanted me to come in as manager of Peterborough, but for my money I had done a pretty good job at Birmingham City, and I felt I could do a job at a higher level (no disrespect to Peterborough United).

Chris was quite poorly at that stage and was in and out of hospital. He called me and said, 'Look, will you come over and see me? I have a proposition for you.' So I went round to see him at his home in Ramsey and he began telling me that the club was running him into the ground and he was struggling to keep himself afloat. He said he had come up with a plan whereby I could run the football side, and whatever money I generated could be spent on bringing in whatever players I liked. That really appealed to me, as I had always been successful in being able to buy players at knock-down prices and sell them on for good money.

He said we'd split the company in two, we'd have a holding company that Chris and Alf Hand would have, and they would then lease me the football side. It's exactly the same deal that CH later did.

Because of my friendship with Chris, I knew the club and its players pretty well. The fact that I would be solely in charge of the football side made me very keen indeed and I thought, 'Well, what harm can it do?' So I came in with a blaze of glory, and me being me I shot my mouth off, saying we'd win the League, we'd score a hundred goals, this that and the other, and in truth that genuinely was my aim.

I came in and I left the board more or less how it was, except Chris, as chairman, had resigned, so he asked me to put Roger Terrell in, which I did. I was told the budget that I had, and I was ready to go.

I got Martin O'Conner for £300,000, Scott Houghton for £80,000, I was putting together a good side. But then the alarm bells started ringing. Iain Russell, the Chief Exec, kept coming to me saying we were short on cash flow and I seemed to be constantly giving him money – £10,000 here, £20,000 there, and it just didn't ring true with me. So I called Chris and I said, 'Look, I'm not happy with things,' and I said I wanted to get my accountant in to check things from top to bottom. My naivety originally was that I didn't do any due diligence when I arrived, which in hindsight I wish I had done.

So Ted Hennessey came in, along with Stephenson Smart Accountants, to go through the accounts. Now whilst this was going on, I had to fly to Scotland to try and do a deal in getting Steve Walsh back to the club. I was having to pay £50,000 through a tribunal for his services. I arrived in Scotland and I get a call from Ted saying they had been through the books and they had found a lot of discrepancies, and that a certain individual had been caught on CCTV stealing money left, right and centre. The police told me to prosecute and maybe I should have, but due to the individual's family circumstances I didn't.

I said to Ted, 'Well I've just been told I've gotta pay £50,000 for Walshey,' to which Ted said, 'I think you need to come back, as this situation is very bad.'

So I flew back to this massive bombshell. In the meantime the bank had frozen the club's accounts, and I now had the responsibility of getting some money into the club. I sold Martin O'Conner to Birmingham for £528,000. They gave me a cheque and I took that to the bank where they then reopened our account. Without that we would never have survived.

So with my big mouth saying we will do this and we will do that, I had brought in all these new players and within a few months I had to sell them all and cut other's wages. Chris was now telling me that my taking over the football side wouldn't work because of tax implications for him and others on the board. It was embarrassing, but because of one thing or another I never actually was owner of Peterborough United. To the outside world that's what I was, but the truth is I never ever was, the whole thing was just a mess.

Really I should have just come out and said, 'Look, you've brought me in here under false pretenses, I'm off,' but I didn't. I had grown to love the club and I wanted to see it come right. I was getting slated by everyone, especially the fans, which I can deal with, but then they never knew the truth. They didn't know that someone had pinched this and pinched that, done this and done that, I actually had my daughter, Amber, come in and take charge of certain areas, which she received allot of stick for from fans and certain staff members which was a fucking disgrace, but Amber took it on the chin, but I needed bring trust back into the building and in fairness to Amber she did far more than what she actually got recognised with and I thank her from the bottom of my heart for the help and assistance that she gave me for all those years, she really is my unsung hero.

I had a good pay-off from Birmingham, which I gave all to my missus. Within three months of me coming into Peterborough I was asking for £10,000 one day, £30,000 the next, and within no time it had all gone, the lot. I hadn't even signed a contract with the club, so I was essentially just throwing my money away. It was horrendous, and keep in mind that at this point I was taking no wages for myself what so ever.

A gentleman called Peter Boizoit then came in to help. I actually met Peter and his nephew up in Soho in London, where they offered to buy the club from me. The thing with Peter is that he is a lovely, lovely man, and for what he has done for the city of Peterborough he deserves a key to the city, he really does. He came to a youth event that we had and after he said it he really enjoyed it. After speaking he saw that I was in trouble, so he invited me to London for a meeting. During the meeting in Soho he said, 'Look, I'll buy the club, but on one condition.' I said, 'Sure, what's that?' 'You stay on and run it!' he said, which was great for me because I just wanted the club to survive and prosper, and I felt that given the right backing I would be the man to do that.

Unfortunately once Peter purchased the club people started coming out of the woodwork and began manipulating him. Many of these people were property developers and wanted the land to build homes on. I got a call from Alf late one night saying that two property developers had arrived at the doorstep and they wanted us to do this, and do that, as Peter Boizoit was going to sell them the club. Alf said, 'Look, we have to do something about it, Peter listens to you.' I said, 'OK, I'll meet you in the car park at 8 o'clock in the morning.'

I met Alf and we went to see Peter. I said to him, 'Peter for all the good you have done for this city, if you sell the club to these people and they wind up the football club and turn the land into houses, the people of Peterborough will make your life a living hell and you don't deserve that!'

In the end he agreed not to sell it to them and he said he would sell it back to myself and Alf, which caused a lot of issues between him and his nephew. But Peter was a man of his word. He wanted £250,000 for it, along with the £1 million overdraft being cleared.

When we came out of the meeting with Peter, Alf said to me, 'Who's gonna give us £250,000 in this short amount of time?' Well, I borrowed the £250,000 from CH. I said to CH, 'Look, as soon as we sell some players and we raise £250k you can have your money back,' and to be fair to CH, he was in his yacht somewhere in the world, but he wired the money across immediately. Within three hours that money was in the club solicitor's account. I don't know how he did it, but he did, and we needed that money quickly to stop those other people from coming in.

However, in hindsight this was the worst thing that I could have done, because now I was effectively renting the club from CH, and this caused its own issues.

I have known CH for about fifteen years, since the day Chris Turner introduced us, and every conversation I had ever had with him was football, football, football. I was fooled into thinking he was just like me, but obviously it turned out that he's not a football nut, and he is nothing like me. He is a ruthless business man and that's why he has made millions and good luck to him, but I couldn't be like that.

After a period of time the relationship between CH and myself changed and he tried to advise me that putting the club into administration was the way forward. Now there are a lot of people who have been good to this football club since I've been here: very loyal, very understanding and very patient. We owed some of them a lot of money, and any of these people could have put writs on us at any point but they didn't, and my promise to them was that I would pay every single penny back. There was no way I was going to let these people suffer and get, nor was I going to allow this football club to go extinct, so I was going to put a real fight in.

In fairness to CH, he let me lease the club off him for a £1 a year. At that time we had the crèche, the bookies, the parole office and the hairdresser's all doing business from the stadium and that was all income, but what I didn't realise until the day I signed the contract was that he had taken all of them away with the holding company, leaving me with no income whatsoever except for the gates and the monies generated from sales. Before I signed the deal, I went to the council and they assured me that a covenant was on the ground so that it could only be used for sporting purposes, and that the land could never be used to build property on. I felt that it was more important that the city had a football club than not, it was better for the community. So this relieved my worries slightly. The wage budget for the football club at that time was around £150,000 a month, and I was again sinking more and more into the shit. I had begged, borrowed and stolen to keep the club in existence. I had even borrowed hundreds of thousands of pounds from David Gold without a single piece of paper being written, and he still says to this day that he never expected to see it again, but I paid David back every single penny, along with everyone else whom the club owed. That makes me very proud, but at this point, trying to find that £150,000 was a massive struggle and was literally making me ill.

I sat the staff down one morning and told them the situation. I said, 'I really don't know how I am going to find everyone's wages this month so I'm asking you to stop your usual day-to-day work and instead work hard in making sure that every penny that is owed to the football club is collected.' However, there was one other opportunity that could help us out... 'Ron Atkinson wants to make a documentary at a football club, warts and all. So much so that these guys will film you taking a shit! But the money generated will pay your wages for the next two months.'

I left it with the staff to decide and straight away they said, 'We don't need time to think about it, we'll do it.' And so *Big Ron Football Manager* came about.

I know it portrayed the club in a bad light and I know people connected with the club and indeed the fans were not happy with the final outcome, but this was about survival. Whether I liked the idea or not, that wasn't a concern, it was just survival and you'll be surprised by the things you would do to survive.

This was such a difficult time for everyone at the club and I really was at my lowest point. People may not believe me when I say this but throughout everything my intentions were good, and always for the benefit of the football club. Everything I had owned and purchased through football I lost trying to keep things afloat. My missus is my best friend and she has always said that she loves me that much that she would live in a tent with me on a field. In all honesty she doesn't know how fucking close she came, seriously.

But every cloud has a silver lining and through the *Big Ron* documentary came Darragh. I call him god, he saved my life, no question about it. Had Darragh MacAnthony not have come into Peterborough United I would be dead now, and I mean that, without a shadow of a doubt. I wasn't eating, I wasn't sleeping. The worry was enormous, and as I said before the responsibility of having to find the wages for the staff was massive. These people didn't just have one job, they had ten, and the money they were being paid was peanuts, but those peanuts were getting harder and harder to find.

So let's get back to my meeting with Darragh's people. I said, 'Look, I want all outstanding debts paid in full.' With this they went away and that was that. I came into the office the next day and Bob Symns said, 'I've had an email from Darragh MacAnthony – he wants to buy the club.' I said, 'Fucking brilliant!' 'He said, he wants to give ya this amount now, this amount in six months, this amount then, etc., etc.' I said, 'What?? Tell him thanks, but I didn't realise it was April Fools Day.'

I never heard anything then for about a month, and in honesty I didn't think any more about it. I had seen that many people now that I wasn't expecting to get a positive response back. And then out of the blue I get a phone call saying, 'Darragh is flying in tomorrow, he wants to meet you.' So the next day came and I was up in the boardroom looking out the window when I saw these three black cars pull into the car park. The doors opened and out stepped five or six blokes in black suits and sunglasses. I sent someone down to bring Darragh up and in came this great big tall guy and the first thing he said was, 'I didn't like that fucking joke about April Fools!' And that was the first thing he said to me. We then sat and talked football, football, football. It was so refreshing to see someone who was actually interested in the football – the ground wasn't mentioned once, and I didn't even know what he did for a living and in honesty I wasn't interested. His knowledge of the game was incredible, it really was: non-League, Football League, foreign leagues, the lot. I showed him around the stadium and as soon as he went out onto the pitch I knew he was sold, we got back in the office and he said, 'I'll buy it.'

The first thing he said was that he wanted to do all the due diligence. I said, 'That's fine, not a problem, but I've been fucked about so many times that I want £150,000 down payment today and its non-refundable, so if you do your due diligence and you pull out, you've lost your money.' He said, 'No problem, I'll have it in your account by this afternoon,' and it fucking was. I've never met a more remarkable man, and one so suited to being a football chairman. He made me wish that he had been around during the thirty one years I had been a manager because he is every manager's dream believe me, however before I was going to accept any deal I made him promise not to sack any of the staff team behind the scenes, to which he agreed and once again he stuck to his word.

Darragh's one failing (and he will admit it) is that he is impatient, and he will tell you that himself. But boy, does he have some bollocks, and he certainly puts his money where his mouth is!

When the deal was completed I called CH, feeling all happy for myself and thinking CH would be pleased for me, etc., etc., but in fact it was the opposite, he went fucking ballistic. He was meant to be my mate, I thought he would have been glad to see me lose this pressure that had been on me. He said, 'I want you to write me a letter to say that whoever takes over the club will give me £750,000 a year rent!' I said, 'Fuck off, I've told him that it would cost him £78,000 a year.' He went crazy at me, it was unbelievable. He got angry, vicious, threatening, the lot.

CH I think was angry because Darragh was a property developer, and I told him straight, I said, 'I didn't even know he was a property developer, all I was interested in was the football. The guy wasn't even interested in the land.' But CH tried everything, and I mean *everything*, to try and make sure this deal didn't go through. I still to this day can't understand for the life of me why it bothered CH so much, because no matter who bought the football side he still owned the ground, so it was no skin off his nose. Whoever came in would only do the same as me and rent it off him.

Darragh was so supportive throughout this, he really was. CH invited Darragh to the Dorchester, and Darragh asked me to come along. KC who was on the board through CH's say so was also at this meeting. We arrived at the Dorchester, CH and Keith were sitting there and then CH began. He said, 'Right Darragh, I know a lot about you, I'm telling you now if you want to buy this football club you can do so through me. Fuck Barry off, 'cos he is nothing to do with it. Don't give him a penny, it will save you a fortune, and just deal with me.'

To be fair to Darragh, and I'll never forget this for as long as I live, he got up, put his hand in his pocket, pulled out some money, put it on the table and walked out of the Dorchester. I got up and followed him. When we got outside he said to me, 'How the fuck can you call that guy in there your friend?' I said, 'I don't know, but I really appreciate what you've just done!'

In fairness to Darragh, that could have saved him a fortune through just dealing with CH, but he didn't, and I am eternally grateful for that.

A few meetings took place between the three of us and at times these became very unfriendly, but Darragh being Darragh stuck to his guns and in the end got his rewards. The Everton game was upon us and I felt there was no better time to introduce my saviour to the fans of Peterborough United, and unveil him as the new chairman of the football club. The deal wasn't done by that point but I stepped down and felt it was the least that Darragh deserved.

Now at that time our manager was Keith Alexander. He was a proper football nut was Keith, a genuinely nice guy. Keith was used to working on shoestring budgets and he was very good at doing so. When Darragh came in offering Keith this, that and the other it sort of blew Keith sideways, he wasn't used to that sort of thing.

The chairman wanted to bring in Izale Mcleod from MK Dons for £1 million and Keith didn't want him. Michael Knightly was another, he was ready to walk in the door but Keith didn't fancy him. We then had a string of results that you wouldn't wish on your worst enemy, and up to this point I was always protecting Keith from Darragh and I was fighting in his corner, but by this stage it was apparent that Darragh wanted his own manager and Keith just didn't want to spend the money that was offered to him. So Darragh asked me to fire Keith, and by this point, considering we hadn't won a match for over a month, I couldn't argue with him.

Remember this was the time of the holy trinity: we spent £250,000 bringing George Boyd into the club, X amount on McLean, a deal had been done securing Mackail-Smith, so money was being spent rapidly and with this came expectations.

Keith knew deep down that this would be coming and he took it really well, in honesty. The chairman, as he always does, honoured Keith's contract, and then it was a case of finding someone to fill those shoes. Tommy Taylor stepped in to manage for a couple of matches as caretaker boss but he was never going to be a permanent fixture.

I remember being in Plymouth sitting in a hotel room when I had a call from Sir Alex Ferguson. He said, 'How are ya?' I said, 'Yeah, not bad, in between managers at the moment but I'm coping.' He said, 'Well, that's what I'm ringing you about, I was ringing to see if you would give my son Darren a shot?'

Now going back to when I was manager of Peterborough, I had tried to sign Darren twice, but I could never get a deal done with Dennis Smith, the Wrexham manager. In fact I also tried signing him from Wolves when I was at Birmingham, because he was such a good midfielder, so I knew plenty about Darren Ferguson.

I said to Alex, 'I will throw his name towards my chairman and I will be in touch, does he not want to stay at Wrexham then?' I asked.

'No, he has been overlooked for the Wrexham job and I think this is your best time to get him' He continued, I said. 'Let me suggest it to my chairman.'

Darren had been at Wrexham for about nine years, and they had just sacked their manager. They were interviewing every man and their dog other than Darren Ferguson, so I went to Darragh and I said, 'I've just had Alex Ferguson on the phone throwing his son's name into the hat. If we can get him as a player/manager that would be fucking brilliant because he would be the best midfielder in the fucking League!"

I knew whilst I was speaking to Darragh that he was googling Darren. He was saying, 'Oh yeah, he's played this amount of games, he's done this and done that,' and all of a sudden he knew more about fucking Darren Ferguson than I did.

He said, 'Yeah, get him in for an interview tomorrow.' I said, 'Woah, woah, woah, he is still a Wrexham player, and I'll need to gain their permission, etc., first.' 'Get it done,' he said, and so I agreed compensation with Wrexham and worked hard in making sure this interview took place.

I called Darren and I said, 'Darren we have a manager's job available and your dad said you might be up for it. It will be a great opportunity for you, we have a new chairman with plenty of money and I've got a feeling you might work well together, do you wanna come in for an interview?'

'Yeah definitely,' Darren said. I said, 'Great – meet me at the club tomorrow and we can discuss things further.' It turned out Darren had a day off that day, so it worked out well. The following day Darren arrived at the club and the pair of us sat down and once again talked football, football, football. He was telling me how he had taken the majority of his coaching badges and he had done a management course at Warwick University – now Darren, the son of Sir Alex, didn't need to do all that, but he was very much his own man and he wanted to do things his way and through his own merit and I don't blame him for that. I called the chairman and then passed the phone over and left them to it. I sat next door in the boardroom with a cup of tea, then another cup, and another cup. An hour later I go through to check if all is OK and he is well away, chatting football with the chairman. It was a pleasure to see.

Darren passed me the phone and I walked back through to the boardroom. I said, 'D. What do you think?' He said, 'What do I think?? Who the fuck was interviewing who there?' I said, 'What do you mean?' He said, 'Well, I told him I wanted back-to-back promotions, to which he replied, "Well what are you gonna do about it?"' Darragh had then said, 'Well what *have* I gotta do about it?' Darren had said, 'Well, you have to get an assistant manager in for me, I want a dietician, a fitness coach, etc., etc.'

I laughed and said, 'OK, what about the money?' He said, 'Money? We didn't mention money once!' I said, 'Really?' He said, 'Yeah, and nor did he mention his dad... Not once.' I said, 'Fuck me, you two are made for each other, it's a match made in heaven!' So Darragh said, 'Offer him the job, and I'll leave the money up to you!'

So I called Darren back in and I said, 'Darragh loves ya, and he wants you to be his first manager of Peterborough United. He said that neither of you mentioned money so we'll need to sort that out.' Darren said, 'I'm not bothered about the money.' I said, 'OK, whatever you're on at

Wrexham, we'll match it and take over your contract,' to which he said, 'Great!' Darren continued by saying he wasn't going to accept the job until he had seen the chairman face to face. I said, 'Oh, fuck me, the chairman's a very impatient man, he won't want to hang about, but I'll give him a call.' So I called the chairman and I told him, he said, 'Barry, I told you to offer him the fucking job!' I said, 'I have offered him the job.' He said, 'Right, he has until 8 o'clock tonight and if he hasn't taken it by one minute past I want you to contact our other choice!' I said, 'Are you having a fucking laugh?' He said, ' No I'm fucking deadly serious,' and he slammed the phone down. I went through to Darren and I said, 'The chairman is that certain he wants you that he wants to offer you the job now, but that window is only open until 8pm!' Darren was shocked by that response, to say the least, but look, knowing Darren as I do now, I know how much he likes to meet people first. He does it with players, he likes to look into their eyes and judge the person he is speaking to and for that there is nothing wrong, but as I said before, the chairman is not a patient man and these were the cards that were on the table.

So Darren said, 'Alright, see ya' and he left. I went from thinking, Wow, this is a done deal, to suddenly not feeling so confident. I went back into the office and I called Darragh I said, 'Look, don't slam the phone down until I've finished.' I said, 'Darren loved the thought of becoming manager, and he was as taken with you as you were with him, but he just wants to meet...' 'Barry, *Barry*!' Darragh interrupted. 'Cut the bullshit. If he wants the job he'll take it, if he don't he won't. I'm not fucking about, I love the guy but he has until 8 o'clock.' Anyway, about 6.30 that evening Alex calls me. He said, 'Barry, Darren's with me, he reckons your chairman's giving him until 8 o'clock to make his mind up on the job.' I said, 'Alex, my man's like that, he's impatient, he's made his mind up and he is sold on Darren, but he won't wait around.' Alex said, 'Well fucking ring him and tell him Darren will take the job.' He passed the phone over to Darren, where we continued our conversation. I immediately contacted the chairman and he was overjoyed, he really was.

The only issue was that I had bigged him up so much about being a great midfielder and that he'd be the best in our League but it turned out he never played a fucking game. But look, it was an incredible signing and it's proved that through the success that the pair of them together have created, so I'm very proud to have been a part of their coming together.

The one thing that Darren Ferguson has is the ability to overachieve. He gets more than the best out of his players, so much so that they would run through a brick wall for him, they really would. He is the model professional. I knew that the pair of them would click, and it takes a certain manager to be able to work under Darragh, it really does. Now I don't mean that in a negative way in any sense, but my chairman has his own way of dealing with situations. I quite like it, but I can see how others would struggle with this.

He can drive you fucking mad, he really can. He would say, 'Offer them £100k.' I'd say, '£100k?? They have turned down £500k already, so why would they accept £100k off little old me, especially spread over five years,' He'd say, 'Director of Football, do your fucking job, or else your cards are waiting.' Now I say that in jest, but that's the kind of way Darragh works. I love talking to the guy, we have some brilliant banter. Even when he's angry, aggressive and demanding, I love the passion, and I say it again, I would have given my bollocks to have had him as chairman, I really would.

I'm fortunate because we bounce off each other and we know exactly how the other one works, it's like second nature.

The only time we have ever had our relationship fray was over the selling of Craig Mackail-Smith. Jim Gannon was manager at the time, and he made it clear to Darragh that he wouldn't be playing Craig any more as he didn't rate him for whatever reason and didn't feel that he was good enough at that level. So I said to Darragh, 'Look, we have a player that you feel is worth £1 million, but at this rate he will be worth two bob if he can't even get in our side.' I said, 'I have a deal on the table from Reading and he is in a hotel there now and will sign the papers tomorrow.' He went fucking ape shit. He said, 'Get him fucking back, fuck the manager, I'm not having Craig go anywhere.'

It's the same as when he went to Norwich, I'm sat there at Carrow Road in the office, they have offered this, offered that, etc., etc., and in fairness it was far more than what we expected in the first place and Darragh said, 'Nah, he ain't going, the fans will think we are a selling club and I ain't having them think that!"

The one and only time we have actually had an argument where I have retaliated was in the summer of 2011, over the same subject. I went over to Cyprus for the chairmen's conference. This is an event that Darragh doesn't have the time to attend so Bob and I usually go over, and it's actually a good place to get deals done. I did six out there last year, and hopefully I'll do fucking thirty this time around! So I usually go for a few days either end of the event and spend some time speaking with different chairmen thrashing out deals and networking in a sense.

Whilst I was over there, Leicester, West Ham and Brighton all approached me over Craig. When I got back in the UK I informed the chairman and we both agreed we would push for West Ham. David Gold is obviously chairman, so I was happy with that completely. I spoke to David Sullivan, the other chairman at West Ham, and he made us an unbelievable offer for Craig. Leicester's offer wasn't so good and Brighton's offer was nowhere near it really.

Anyway Craig went to see Sam at West Ham and Sven at Leicester and he didn't pick up good vibes from either. With West Ham the club would have got the best money and Craig would have got the best money, but Craig is all about the football. He's a good lad, and he didn't feel he would play much under either of those managers, so he decided on Brighton given the fact that Gus Poyet told him that he would build a team around him.

The chairman and I had a big row over this. Darragh couldn't understand why Craig was choosing Brighton over the other two and he sort of intimated that I had been looking out for what was best for Craig rather than what was best for the club on the back of Craig being in a relationship with my daughter Amber. I went ape shit with him on that, because I would never do that and especially with Darragh, because of what I owed to him personally for all that he had done for me. I would never go against him in a million years, never.

I even went round Craig's house and told him he was mad, West Ham would definitely return to the Prem and it could be a fantastic move. But as I said, in fairness to Craig he just wanted to play football and he felt that Brighton was that right move.

It was a horrible row, it really was, but I was never going to be accused of something that wasn't true. In the end Leicester waited a month from their original conversation with Craig to actually making further contact, and Big Sam at West Ham felt that the offer made was a bit too rich so it turned out that the only offer left on the table at the end was Brighton's, which it just so happened was Craig's preferred choice. Brighton paid £2.5 million up front plus add-ons so it wasn't all bad, was it?

The one thing that the chairman can't get his head round is that if a player has a host of clubs to choose from, it's the player that gets the choice, because if the player isn't happy about joining the team he won't sign and for that deal to go through you need the player's signature. So it doesn't matter if the club is offered £1 million, £3 million or even £10 million, if the player doesn't want to go then we're fucked. But that is football and that is how it is.

But that genuinely was our one and only argument to this date and hopefully that's how it will stay. But look, it's not all been easy for Darragh, not by any stretch of the imagination. The period of Darren's exit was a horrendous time, and I could see how much it was hurting him, I really could. The first time I smelt a rat was when the gaffer arranged a match with Histon to take a look at a few trialists. I got to the match and there was no sign of the gaffer. Rooster appeared for a while but didn't stay till the end. The chairman rang me and said, 'What did the gaffer think of the players?' I said, 'I don't know, the gaffer isn't here.' What do you mean?' he said. 'Rooster was here earlier but the gaffer hasn't shown,' I said.

Anyway I got in my car and drove home and I got another call from the chairman. 'Where's the gaffer?' he said. I said, 'I told you an hour ago I ain't got a fucking clue.' 'Well I've just read on the message boards that he's in Leeds having dinner with the Hull City chairman Adam Pearson!'

I said, 'Darragh, I've told you about them fucking message boards. Steer clear of those fucking things, it's all bullshit.'

Anyway, the week leading up to the Newcastle game the gaffer did a few things that were a bit strange in my opinion. Firstly he gave the lads a couple of days off. We had just lost to the bottom of the table and we were now facing the top of the table in Newcastle United. I felt it was very unlike Darren to give the guys a few days off before such a big match.

The day of the match I met Darragh at the hotel and he said, 'Do you know the team?' I said, 'No I ain't got a clue.' He said, 'He has left Aaron out!" I couldn't believe what I was hearing, it absolutely bowled me over. The lads began making their way over to the coach and I could see Darragh having a few words with Aaron. Darragh then came back over telling me that Aaron wanted to get in a cab and fuck off home, he'd had enough and couldn't believe he was on the bench for the biggest game of his career. The chairman told him to keep his head up, focus on the task ahead and if he was called upon to make his mark in the game by grabbing some goals.

It seemed strange to me that Aaron had only been told the morning of the match, given that usually the team spend all week working on the shape for the forthcoming fixture, but then again the fact that they had had the time off in the week would have messed all those plans up. It was all very confusing and the chairman was panicking big time.

A fortnight previously the chairman had brought in two players on Darren's request, Ryan Bennett for £500,000, and Scott Griffiths for £125,000. This was a lot of money spent on the manager's wishes, so at no stage did the chairman feel that the end was imminent.

The chairman said, 'Come on, it's a big game, let's go on the coach and enjoy the day.' This was a chance for Darragh to be a visiting chairman in a fantastic ground like St James Park. In fairness no one was expecting a shock result that day, and we lost the match 3-1 which for me showed we gave it a good go.

After the match we all went our separate ways and made our way home, and about an hour or so into my journey I had a call from the chairman saying, 'Have you spoken to the gaffer? He hasn't called me.' I said, 'No, but it's a four-hour journey from Newcastle to Peterborough, so there's plenty of time.' I got home and it was about 10pm by this point and I got another call. 'Have you heard from the gaffer?' I said 'No.' He said, 'I'm getting a bad feeling about this.' I said, 'Darragh, the only reason you're getting a bad feeling is because of this shit you read on the message boards.' I said, 'Look, OK, I'll ring Adam Pearson.'

I called Adam Pearson and I said, 'Adam how are ya, mate? There is nonsense circulating that you've had dinner with our gaffer and my fucking chairman ain't happy!' He said, 'Barry, are you off your fucking rocker? I haven't had a conversation with Darren Ferguson at all!" I said, 'Fine, sorry to disturb ya.' I then called Darragh back and explained the call and Darragh said, 'Nah, bollocks, I don't believe it.' I said, 'I do, they have to deal with us, it's written in his contract, so relax.'

This was all ridiculous, we had gone from heaven to hell in the matter of months and the chairman was feeling more and more paranoid by the day and I wanted to reassure him and protect him.

This Saturday night though he rings me again about 12.30 and by this time he was really upset. I was meant to be going over to David Gold's that evening, but I told him I would be going over in the morning instead. I said, 'Look, I'm going to David Gold's for Sunday lunch tomorrow, and I will be back at the club Monday, but before I leave for David's I will go via the ground in the morning and see the gaffer to see what's going on.'

I got to the ground at 10am and the place was locked. This knocked me back because the ground is always open on a Sunday as the gaffer usually has the players in for a warm down, or at the very least the injured players would be in with the physio, but there was no sight of anybody.

I called the gaffer and his wife answered. I said, 'Is the gaffer there?' She said, 'He's in bed.' I said, 'Can ya get him up?' 'Not really,' she said.

'OK, when Darren gets up can you ask him to give me a call, I'm down at the ground and I was expecting to see him with the players having a warm down.'

In fairness to Darren he called me back within twenty minutes.

He said 'What's up?' I said, 'I'm concerned 'cos you haven't called the chairman, and you're not at the club.' He said, 'Nah.' So I said, 'Well look, I need to see ya, Darren.' He said, 'OK, no problem I'll meet you on the A1.'

I met him and I said, 'Darren, you want the fucking sack, mate?' He said, 'You're fucking mad, what makes you think that?'

I said, 'Well, there are loads of odd things. You weren't at Histon to watch the trialists, you left Aaron out of the side against Newcastle, there is shit circulating that you've met Adam Pearson, and now you're not ringing the chairman, which is unusual.'

He said, 'Look, I'll speak to the chairman, I've got a list of players I need to speak to him about anyway.'

I said, 'OK, well I'm off to David Gold's and the chairman is flying between 1 and 3 so don't ring him then.' He said, 'Nah, I'll ring him when I get home, I'll ring him straight away.'

So I got back in my car, and I called the chairman and I said, 'Chairman, I've just spoken with the gaffer and everything is fine. I told him I felt he was being tapped up and that he wanted the sack and he told me I was crazy. He then showed me a list of players that he had in mind, so all is good and he will ring you shortly.' 'No probs, thanks Baz,' he said.

Anyway I get to David Gold's and we had a late lunch and we relaxed through the afternoon. We then had a dinner party in the evening with about twelve other people. I was sitting there and I got a phone call from the chairman: 'Baz, I thought you said the gaffer was gonna ring me?' I said, 'He ain't rang ya yet?' 'Nope,' he replied. I said 'OK, I'll ring him.' 'No, ya won't,' he said, and he hung up on me. Now at this point I wasn't able to settle or enjoy my evening at all and my mind was with Darragh and the pain he was going through. I mean this was tearing him apart. I was meant to be staying over that night but I told my missus I was going back to sort this out. In the meantime Darragh calls me again, even more pissed off than before. He said, 'He obviously wants to go, doesn't he?' I said, 'Chairman, I'll finish my coffee and I'll get on my way, and I'll meet the manager at 8 o'clock in the morning.'

So I got to the ground at 8 o'clock and I said to the gaffer, 'I thought you were gonna ring the chairman?' He said, 'Yeah, I know.' I said, 'Well why didn't ya?' He leaned across the desk and said, 'HE'S GOT MY FUCKING NUMBER, HE CAN FUCKING RING ME, CAN'T HE?' He really snapped.

I said, 'Fuck me Darren, we've gotta part ways mate,' and that was the start. From that, within half an hour we had the Ferguson lawyers from Aberdeen on the phone, a deal was made, and Darren was no longer manager of Peterborough United Football Club.

I still can't quite believe it to this day. It was just so sad and so unnecessary. These two guys that had created so much success were just refusing to speak to each other. The last thing I said to Darren when he left was no matter how long he is involved in the game, he will never have another chairman like Darragh MacAnthony.

The thing that really annoyed me was the fact that Rooster then handed in his resignation and shortly afterwards Scott Taylor, our fitness coach, followed. Now to me you wouldn't be doing that unless you had another job lined up, that was my opinion.

Darragh created a list of possible replacements and he was flying in for a press conference on the Monday. This whole situation was a bad one and during the press conference Darragh was getting hammered by the press. My problem was that these guys didn't have a clue about what really happened and they were accusing the chairman of this that and the other so I just took over and said, 'He's been tapped up' and that's how I felt, in fairness. I've since apologised to Darren for that and I was out of order, it caused a rift between myself, Darren and his father. But I was just fed up with seeing these guys banging in to the chairman for something that wasn't his fault, so I had to say something. The situation hurt me and I wish that I had just banged their heads together at the time and made them see sense. It was childish, the whole situation.

From that point on we were Ragarse Rovers, which was very sad. We interviewed Pat Fenlon and we came very close to offering him the job until his agent stepped in asking for the moon on a stick. I said, 'Fucking hell, mate, we're Peterborough United not Manchester United.' The chairman then changed his mind and took the offer from the table and in fact Pat called us up later that evening saying 'Look, take my agent out of the situation, I want the job,' I said, 'Pat it's too late, mate, the chairman has taken the deal off the table.'

We then brought Mark Cooper in which in fairness was the wrong decision. The guy interviewed incredibly well, but he had the impossible task of filling the boots of Darren Ferguson. I say to people now, whoever takes the Man Utd job after Sir Alex I will feel really sorry for, it's not that job you want, it's the one after that, because you will always live in your predecessor's shadow. That's just a fact of life, and this was the same for Mark Cooper.

Jim Gannon was a stop-gap. For my money he was never going to take the job full time. He is a man that is about ten years ahead of his time and I know the chairman liked him a lot but Jim just didn't want the job full time and you have to respect that.

And then came Gary Johnson, a massively experienced guy but for one reason or another the chairman and Gary just didn't connect, and that connection is vitally important. Gary's not stupid either. Everything the chairman mentioned had some reference to Darren Ferguson and I think deep down Gary knew that if anything was to happen between Darren and Preston then there would be a strong possibility of Darren returning.

Gary's pitfall was the Brighton match, where he nearly resigned at half time. Doing that is the quickest way to lose your dressing room and unfortunately for Gary that's what happened.

The period as a whole was so difficult for the chairman, and I am sure it's a period that he would like to forget. But a valuable lesson was learnt through that devastation that benefited everyone involved: they learnt that the grass isn't greener.

We made mistakes, and it was out there for the world to see, but we are human. It's OK to make mistakes, but it's how you learn from those mistakes that's important, and I truly believe we have, every one of us.

When Darren left us, I spoke in length with the chairman of Preston and Sheffield Wednesday who were both looking for managers at the time, and I gave him a glowing reference.

In the time he was manager at Preston we had spoke once or twice, but himself and the chairman had not spoke a word since Newcastle. When Darren was sacked from Preston the chairman asked me if I could arrange a meeting between the three of us, and I told him no, it is the one and only time I have ever said that word to him. I told him that the issues were with Darren and himself and that they needed to sort out their differences alone. I asked Clive who is Darrens agent to meet the chairman and I left it at that.

Darragh invited Darren to London Road to watch us play Brentford in the league and when he walked back into the building his first words to me were 'You were right about me having no better chairman!'

Looking back now it was yet another master stroke from Darragh MacAnthony. It was an emotional return, in fairness, and the pair just wanted to get back to work immediately.

The result of this master stroke was the play-off final, a match that will live with me and I'm sure many others for a very long time. The fact that it was at Old Trafford was like a dream come true – but the combination of these two back together showed that success is the result of that formula and long may it continue.

STATISTICS

GAME BREAKDOWN

Home

	P	W	D	L	F	A	Pts
League	134	67	29	38	257	187	230
FA cup	8	3	2	3	12	10	
L cup	9	5	0	4	14	13	
Others	3	2	0	1	3	1	
Total	154	77	31	46	286	211	

Away

	P	W	D	L	F	A	Pts
League	133	45	30	58	172	192	165
FA cup	11	6	2	3	20	17	
L cup	4	2	0	2	11	10	
Others	6	2	0	4	11	12	
Total	154	55	32	67	214	231	

Total

	P	W	D	L	F	A	Pts
League	267	112	59	96	429	379	395
FA cup	19	9	4	6	32	27	
L cup	13	7	0	6	25	23	
Others	9	4	0	5	14	13	
Total	308	132	63	113	500	442	
		43%	20%	37%	1.62	1.43	

MY MANAGERS

2006-2007	Keith Alexander
2007	Tommy Taylor (C/T)
2007-2009	Darren Ferguson
2009-2010	Mark Cooper
2010	Jim Gannon
2010-2011	Gary Johnson
2011	David Oldfield (C/T)
2011-Present	Darren Ferguson

THE GATES

Season	Games	Total	Ave
06/07	19	88,347	4,650
07/08	23	137,988	5,999
08/09	23	174,823	7,601
09/10	23	205,014	8,914
10/11	23	147,610	6,418
11/12	23	211,614	9,201

SEASON ENDING

2007/08	Promoted
2008/09	Promoted
2009/10	Relegated
2010/11	Promoted
2011/12	18th in the Championship

CLUB RECORDS

Highest scoring win

Peterborough United 8 Oldham Athletic 1, 26.11.1969

Peterborough United 8 Accrington Stanley 2, 15.01.2008

Highest winning margin

Peterborough United 8 Oldham Athletic 1, 26.11.1969

Peterborough United 7 Barrow 0, 09.10.1971

Peterborough United 7 Brentford 0, 24.11.2007

Highest scoring draw

Peterborough United 4 Swansea City 4, 03.12.1966

Peterborough United 4 Lincoln City 4, 12.02.1972

Peterborough United 4 Hartlepool United 4, 27.02.1982

Peterborough United 4 Cardiff City 4, 28.12.2009

Peterborough United 4 Southampton 4, 05.02.2011

Money Spent on Transfers

From October 2006 – May 2012 **£7,824,337**

Money Received from Transfers

From October 2006 – May 2012 **£9,771,093**

DID YOU KNOW?

Peterborough United finished the 2010/11 season as the highest scoring team in the country with 106 League goals. 28 goals more than Premier League champions Manchester United.

George Boyd signing from Stevenage in 2007 was a Conference record at the time of £260,000.

The 2011 purchase of Tyrone Barnett from Crawley Town was the club's first £1 million signing.

HIGHEST TRANSFER FEES PAID
(INCLUDING ADD ON'S)

1. Tyrone Barnett (over £1,100,000 from Crawley Town, 8th May 2012)

2. Ryan Bennett (£1,000,000 from Grimsby Town, 15th January 2010)

3. Joe Lewis (£510,000 from Norwich City, 8th January 2008)

4. Gabriel Zakuani (£400,000 from Fulham, 2nd January 2009)

5. Martin O'Connor (£350,000 from Walsall, 5th July 1996)

6. Nicky Ajose (£300,000 from Manchester Utd, 5th July 2011)

7. Shaun Brisley (£300,000 from Macclesfield Town, 8th May 2012)

8. Toumani Diagouraga (£300,000 from Hereford Utd, 17th June 2009)

9. George Boyd (£296,000 from Stevenage, 8th January 2007)

10. Tommy Rowe (£275,000 from Stockport County, 11th May 2009)

11. Howard Forinton (£250,000 from Birmingham City, 17th September 1999)

12. Carl Griffiths (£225,000 from Portsmouth, 28th March 1996)

13. Lee Frecklington (£200,000 from Lincoln City, 15th May 2009)

14. Lee Tomlin (£180,000 from Rushden & Diamonds, 9th August 2010)

15. Ken Charlery (£170,000 from Watford, 16th December 1993)

16. Scott Griffiths (£150,000 from Dagenham & Redbridge, 15th January 2010)

17. Dominic Green (£150,000 from Dagenham & Redbridge, 27th August 2008)

18. Liam Hatch (£150,000 from Barnet, 1st January 2008)

19. Aaron McLean (£150,000 from Grays Ath., 1st January 2007)

20. Ken Charlery (£150,000 from Birmingham City)

HIGHEST TRANSFER FEES RECEIVED
(INCLUDING ADD ONS)

1. Ryan Bennett (over £3,000,000 to Norwich City, 31st January 2012)

2. Craig Mackail-Smith (over £3,000,000 to Brighton, 4th July 2011)

3. Aaron McLean (£1,300,000 to Hull City, 1st January 2011)

4. Simon Davies (£700,000 to Tottenham Hotspur, 10th January 2000)

5. David Billington (£500,000 to Sheffield Wednesday, 27th March 1997)

6. Paul Coutts (£500,000 to Preston North End, 2nd February 2010)

7. Adam Drury (£500,000 to Norwich City, 21st March 2001)

8. Matthew Etherington (£500,000 to Tottenham Hotspur, 10th January 2000)

9. Mark McKeever (£500,000 to Sheffield Wednesday, 31st March 1997)

10. Martin O'Connor (£500,000 to Birmingham City, 29th November 1996)

11. Luke Steele (£500,000 to Manchester Utd, 11th May 2002)

12. Craig Morgan (£400,000 to Preston North End, 6th July 2010)

13. Dave Robinson (£400,000 to Notts County, 11th September 1992)

14. Ken Charlery (£350,000 to Watford, 15th October 1992)

15. Ken Charlery (£350,000 to Birmingham City, 3rd July 1995)

16. Tom Williams (£350,000 to Birmingham City, 13th March 2002)

17. Ian Bennett (£325,000 to Birmingham City, 17th December 1993)

18. Leon McKenzie (£325,000 to Norwich City)

19. Shaun Batt (£300,000 to Millwall, 15th June 2010)

20. Jimmy Bullard (£275,000 to Wigan Ath., 31st January 2003)

PLAYERS IN AND OUT UNDER MY TIME

PLAYERS STILL AT POSH

Adjei-Kyem	Gaughran	McKeown	Webb
Agard	Geohaghon	McLean	Wesolowski
Amos	Gilbert	McLeod	Westwood
Andrew	Gill	Mendez Laing	Whelpdale
Appiah	Gnapka	Mills	White
Basey	Gorden	Mitchell	Williams
Batt	Green	Morgen	Wotton
Bennett	Hatch	Nyatanga	Wright
Blackett	Hicks	Obika	
Blanchett	Howe	Ofori-Twumasi	
Briggs	Hughes	Pearce	
Charnock	Hyde	Piergianni	
Chester	Jalal	Potter	
Clayton	Keates	Rachubka	
Cole	Kennedy	Reid	
Collis	Koranteng	Rendell	
Coutts	Langmead	Richardson	
Crofts	Lee	Rose	
Crook	Lewis	Simpson	
Davies	Livermore	Smith	
Davies	Low	Strachan	
Diagouraga	Mackail-Smith	Thompson	
Dickinson	Martin	Torres	
Dove	McCrae	Tunnicliffe	

Ajose	Jones
Alcock	Kearns
Ball	Lawler
Barnett	Little
Boyd	McCann
Brisley	Newell
Coulson	Nthle
Day	Ralph
Frecklington	Rowe
Gordon-Hutton	Sinclair
Grant	Taylor
Griffiths	Tomlin
Hibbert	Zakuani

PLAYERS RELEASED BUT NOT PURCHASED BY ME

Arber	Huke
Benjamin	McShane
Branston	Newton
Butcher	Opara
Carden	Plummer
Crow	Richards
Day	Stirling
Fry	Turner
Futhcer	Tyler
Gain	Williams
Chaichem	Yeo
Holden	

THE HOLY TRINITY

AARON MCLEAN

Aaron McLean had his best statistical year in Peterborough United's 2007–08 campaign, which resulted in the clubs promotion into League One. McLean scored 29 goals in the league in 45 appearances that season, which made him the League's leading scorer and earned him the League Two Golden Boot. He also scored three goals in four FA Cup appearances that year. Aaron scored a total of 83 goals from 178 appearances.

CRAIG MACKAIL-SMITH

Craig Mackail Smith managed to rack up 35 goals for the club during the 2010–11 season. Those 35 goals made him the most prolific scorer in England for the season and also bagged him the coveted prize of Football League One Player of the Year Award and also the League One Golden Boot. Craig scored a total of 99 goals for Posh from 198 appearances.

GEORGE BOYD

In October 2009, Boyd made a club record-equalling 124th consecutive appearance. He was named in the League Two 2008 PFA Team of the Year. Boyd was also named in the League One 2009 PFA Team of the Year the following season for the second successive year. George scored 68 goals from 256 appearances.